"I wish this book had been around when I was an atheist and started to seek God. It's a no-nonsense, practical, and insightful guide that will help all those on a quest for spiritual truth. If you're investigating whether there's any substance to the Christian faith, you must read this important book."

Lee Strobel, former award-winning legal editor of the *Chicago Tribune* and bestselling author of more than twenty books

CHRISTIANITY
FOR PEOPLE
WHO AREN'T
CHRISTIANS

CHRISTIANITY
FOR PEOPLE
WHO AREN'T
CHRISTIANS

UNCOMMON ANSWERS
TO COMMON QUESTIONS

JAMES EMERY WHITE

BakerBooks
a division of Baker Publishing Group
Grand Rapids, Michigan

Published by Baker Books
a division of Baker Publishing Group
PO Box 6287, Grand Rapids, MI 49516-6287
www.bakerbooks.com

Printed in the United States of America

Library of Congress Cataloging-in-Publication Data
Names: White, James Emery, 1961– author.
Title: Christianity for people who aren't Christians : uncommon answers to
    common questions / James Emery White.
Description: Grand Rapids : Baker Books, a division of Baker Publishing Group,
    2019. | Includes bibliographical references.
Identifiers: LCCN 2019003829 | ISBN 9780801094590 (pbk.)
Subjects: LCSH: Apologetics. | Christianity—Essence, genius, nature.
Classification: LCC BT1103 .W475 2019 | DDC 239—dc23
LC record available at https://lccn.loc.gov/2019003829

19 20 21 22 23 24 25   7 6 5 4 3 2 1

CONTENTS

ACKNOWLEDGMENTS

I wish to thank the Baker team for their support of this project, our seventh together, and specifically Bob Hosack, who connected with the idea and vision of this book almost immediately.

Alli Main is one of the great gifts to my life and earns my deepest gratitude for her assistance with all of my writing. Whether through research or editing, feedback or ideas, constructive criticism or encouragement, she is nothing less than a godsend.

And as always, my wife, Susan, continues to make every page possible. After thirty-five years of marriage, I think it's safe to say she is still the love of my life.

Finally, to Mecklenburg Community Church, an amazing community of people who continue to die to themselves daily in countless ways in order to reach out to their friends and family, neighbors and coworkers, and share the message of the Christian faith like gossip over the backyard fence. It's an honor to be your pastor.

INTRODUCTION

We are half-hearted creatures, fooling around with drink and sex and ambition, when infinite joy is offered us . . . like an ignorant child who wants to go on making mud pies in a slum because he cannot imagine what is meant by the offer of a holiday by the sea. We are far too easily pleased.

C. S. Lewis, "The Weight of Glory"

Men despise religion; they hate it, and fear it is true.

Pascal, *Pensées*

I hope you begin this book with a healthy amount of doubt. It's the best way to explore anything. When you believe something to be true, you are "in one mind" about accepting it; when you do not believe something to be true, you are "in one mind" about rejecting it. "To doubt," Os Guinness writes, "is to waver between the two, to believe and disbelieve at once and to be 'in two minds.'"[1]

I'm so glad someone gave me that permission. When I was around nine, it dawned on me that the reason I considered myself a Christian was because my parents were Christians. Like a

11

thunderbolt from the blue it hit me: *That's why I believe all of this—I have been* raised *to believe it all!* Which, of course, did not make it true. My preadolescent brain quickly surmised that if I had been born in India, I would have been raised a Hindu. It would have been Hinduism I believed and accepted. If I had been born in Iran, my parents would have raised me to accept the Muslim faith. If I had been raised in Pittsburgh, my parents would have raised me to accept the cult known as "Steeler Nation" and I would be waving yellow towels in worship.

I remember panicking—what if I wasn't born in the right place? My entire eternity suddenly seemed to rest on whether my family of origin was geographically correct.

I went to my mother, innocently working in the kitchen and unaware of my spiritual crisis, and asked, "Mom, why are we Christians? You did . . . like . . . check it out first, didn't you? How do you know we're believing the right thing?" I then shared my geographical concerns. She did not dismiss me or give me a quick "Don't worry" kind of reply that would have trivialized my question. She knew me well enough to know that I was serious about the question.

So she did something that was very unusual for a parent to do for their nine-year-old son. She said, "Jim, your father and I have looked at all of the faiths of the world and have determined that Christianity is true. It's not just about where we live—Christians are all over the world and, in fact, it's the world's largest faith. You'll find Christians in India, in Iran, and other places as well, so it's not just about geography. But you have to come to that in your own mind. So you are welcome to look into all of the world's religions and come to your own conclusions. And if, at the end, you want to go to a different church, or believe something else, or believe in nothing at all, that is your choice."

When she said that to me, I heaved a huge sigh of relief. Not just because they had apparently done their homework, but also because I was allowed to pursue my questions without fear of retribution. Without insecurity. There was something comforting—even reassuring—about such freedom. I learned that questions, by themselves, were not wrong. Neither was good, solid, healthy doubt, which can be the fuel that energizes any faith when seeking understanding.

It was many years before I settled the matter for my own life, so I know what it's like to approach the Christian faith (or any faith, for that matter) with a healthy dose of skepticism, curiosity, willful disobedience, and, for my part, ignorance. Which is why this is a book about the Christian faith for people who may not be Christians, written by someone who understands not being one. As such, I will try to accomplish two things: first, to explain the Christian faith in a way that doesn't assume you have a foundational knowledge or understanding of it. I'm not going to assume you were raised in a church or that you've had much exposure to the Christian faith. Second, I'd like to try to answer some of the more common questions people standing outside of the Christian faith are quite reasonable to ask based on what they *do* know or understand about it. And I think you'll find these answers are uncommon—meaning they may not be the answers you'd expect based on caricatures or ideas you've already formed about Christians. If you consider yourself a Christian, I've got a feeling you'll enjoy this conversation, too, as there may be many aspects of the Christian faith you've never fully understood or questions that have remained unanswered. You can have doubts even as you believe.

It won't just be you and me on this journey. You will find that I have invited a partner to join me. His name is C. S. Lewis. He died on the same day as John F. Kennedy and Aldous Huxley, so he's not exactly a contemporary. I mention him because you will find that as we walk through the Christian faith, I bring him up from time to time. One reason is that his writing and thinking were very helpful to me when I first explored the Christian faith. The second reason is that he also understands what it's like to be an atheist well into his adult life.

If you're not familiar with Lewis, you may be familiar with some of his friends, particularly J. R. R. Tolkien of *The Lord of the Rings* fame. They spent many, many hours together at their favorite Oxford pub, The Eagle and Child (affectionately known by locals as "The Bird and the Baby"). As a plaque on the wall reads:

> C. S. Lewis, his brother, W. H. Lewis, J.R.R. Tolkien, Charles Williams and other friends met every Tuesday morning, between the years 1939–1962 in the back room of this their favorite pub. These men, popularly known as the "Inklings," met here to drink beer and to discuss, among other things, the books they were writing.

Wikimedia Commons

The Eagle and Child pub in Oxford, England

If you are familiar with Lewis, it is probably as a result of the movie of his life titled *Shadowlands*, his seven-volume *Chronicles of Narnia* (also made into movies), and such works as *The Screwtape Letters* and *Mere Christianity*.

Lewis went to University College, Oxford, where he achieved a rare double first in Classics, an additional first in English, and the Chancellor's Prize for academics. He was shortly offered a teaching position at Magdalen College, Oxford, where he was a fellow and tutor from 1925–54, and then later at the University of Cambridge as professor of Medieval and Renaissance English from 1954–63.[2] In 1931, Lewis came out of atheism into the Christian faith, aided significantly through his friendship with Tolkien. As he journeyed away from his rejection of any type of God, he flirted with several alternate worldviews before Christianity—most seriously Hinduism—but ended with Jesus. But this journey was not without resistance. On the particular day in the Trinity Term of 1929 when he "gave in, and admitted that God was God, and knelt and prayed," he confessed he did so as "the most reluctant convert in all of England."[3]

The intellectual questions that plagued him during his spiritual journey—why God allows pain and suffering, how Christianity can be the one and only way to God, the place of miracles— became the very questions he later navigated with such skill. They were my questions too.

I'm also drawn to Lewis because—while thoroughly converted—he didn't act the way some would say Christians are "supposed to" act. It has been suggested that he could not even be hired by the evangelical college that now stewards his personal letters due to his pipe-smoking, ale-drinking, free-speaking ways. Do you remember what the plaque at The Eagle and Child said they would do when they met at the pub? *Drink beer.* And do you remember what time it said they often met? *In the morning.* I've spent time at Oxford pursuing various post-doctoral studies. Over many years, in my many hours at The Eagle and Child pub,

I've had conversations with people who knew Lewis. I have heard tales of how he would often come to class with alcohol on his breath—sometimes with what we might call a bit of a "buzz." No, not drunk, but without a doubt having clearly imbibed. I was told that he had holes in his coat pockets from putting away his pipe and the ashes burning through. He was also widely known to be loud and somewhat earthy in his stories.[4]

I think we would have liked him.

Addison's Walk

There is a path on the grounds of Magdalen College where Lewis taught, just a short ways from Merton College where Tolkien resided, called Addison's Walk. The path runs beside several streams of the River Cherwell. On Saturday, September 19, 1931, Lewis invited two friends to dine with him in his rooms at Magdalen. One was a man by the name of Hugo Dyson, a lecturer in English Literature at Reading University. The other was Tolkien.

On that fall evening, after they had dined, Lewis took his guests on a walk through the Magdalen grounds, ending with a stroll down Addison's Walk. It was there they began to discuss the idea of metaphor and myth. Lewis had long appreciated myth. As a boy, he loved the great Norse stories of the dying god Balder; and as a man, he grew to love and appreciate the power of myth throughout the history of language and literature. But he didn't *believe* in them. Beautiful and moving though they might be, they were, he concluded, ultimately untrue. As he expressed to Tolkien, myths are "lies and therefore worthless, even though breathed through silver."

"No," said Tolkien. "They are not lies."

Later, Lewis recalled that at the moment Tolkien uttered those words, "a rush of wind . . . came so suddenly on the still, warm evening and sent so many leaves pattering down that we thought it was raining. We held our breath."

Addison's Walk at Magdalen College, Oxford, England

Tolkien's point was that the great myths might just reflect a splintered fragment of the true light. Within the myth, there was something of eternal truth. They talked on, and Lewis became convinced by the force of Tolkien's argument. They returned to Lewis's rooms on Staircase III of New Building. Once there, they turned their conversation to Christianity. In the case of Christianity, Tolkien argued, the poet who invented the story was none other than God himself, and the images he used were real men and women and actual history.

Lewis was floored.

"Do you mean," he asked, "that the death and resurrection of Christ is the old 'dying God' story all over again?"

Yes, Tolkien answered, except that here is a *real* "dying" God, with a precise location in history and definite historical consequences. The old myth has become fact. Such joining of faith and intellect had never occurred to Lewis.

The time approached 3:00 a.m. and Tolkien had to go home. Lewis and Dyson escorted him down the stairs. They crossed the

17

quadrangle and let him out by the little postern gate on Magdalen Bridge. Lewis remembered that "Dyson and I found more to say to one another, strolling up and down the cloister of New Building, so that we did not get to bed till 4."

Twelve days later, Lewis wrote to his close boyhood friend Arthur Greeves: "I have just passed on from believing in God to definitely believing in Christ—in Christianity. I will try to explain this another time. My long night talk with Dyson and Tolkien had a good deal to do with it."[5]

So let's go on a long walk together. You may not land where Lewis did, but hopefully the journey itself will prove enlightening.

1

THE GOD WHO IS THERE
... OR NOT

If God did not exist it would be necessary to invent him.

Voltaire, *Epitre a l'Auteru du Livre des Trois Imposteurs*

If you don't care about the interplay between science and matters of faith, or if you already believe in God, feel free to skip this chapter. If the interplay between science and faith *is* important to you, and you're not at all sure whether you believe in God, then let's begin.

On August 7, 1961, a twenty-six-year-old Russian cosmonaut became the second Soviet to fire off into space, orbit the earth, and return safely. When he returned, he let it be known that while in space, he looked around for this God people talked about and couldn't see him.

While some do see things that way, there aren't too many card-carrying atheists in the world. Recent polls show that 80 percent of all Americans believe in the existence of God. If you throw in those who may shy away from the word "God," but who would say they believe in a "higher power," the percentage increases to nearly 90 percent. But when it comes to the God of the *Bible*, the percentages drop dramatically.[1] Let's just say that there are an understandably healthy number of agnostics out there, and you might put yourself among them. An agnostic doesn't necessarily reject God himself as much as the possibility of *knowing* whether God exists. Rather than say, "I *don't* know if there is a God," they say, "I *cannot* know if there is a God." Or, even beyond that, which God.

So let's start with whether a God even exists. The Christian faith very much believes in a God who is there and—as the famed Christian thinker Francis Schaeffer added—has not been silent. But why would a thinking person believe such a thing? Can the existence of God be proven? Obviously, you cannot put God into a test tube for examination. You cannot prove that God exists, at least by normal scientific methods, because the scientific method depends upon repetition. There are certain things that cannot be contained or repeated in order to be scientifically proven. If something cannot be examined beyond our five senses, then you cannot use science to either prove or disprove it. However, just because you can't repeat something doesn't mean it isn't real. No one has ever seen love, but we all know it is real. No one has ever smelled freedom, but it exists. And, of course, God—by almost any definition—would be very hard to examine by human measures. So instead of a chemical reaction in a test tube that would somehow reveal God's existence, those who are wanting Christians to explain their belief should instead look for evidence that would support whether it is *reasonable* to believe in the existence of God: signs, if you will, of his existence. Christians believe that such evidence exists in abundance, beginning with something as simple as cause and effect.

Cause and Effect

Most of us have ventured out on a clear night to look up and stare at the stars. During moments like those, it is natural to reflect not only on the vastness of the universe, but to wonder how it came into being.

Only recently has the idea that the world was created by a personal God been dismissed by some as intellectually absurd. The late-coming idea is that there was no creative event at all. The late astronomer Carl Sagan opened up his bestselling book *Cosmos* by saying, "The cosmos is all that is or ever was or ever will be."[2] But the most recent findings of science are turning us back to—if not a God—the reality of a creation event. For example, the second law of thermodynamics states that the universe is running out of usable energy. And if it is running *out* of energy, then it cannot be eternal and must have at one time been given an initial "start" of energy. Something does not wind down unless it has been wound *up*.

These ideas related to the second law of thermodynamics have been supported through the leading hypothesis for the beginning

Unsplash

Picture of the mountains and stars at Fiordland National Park, New Zealand

of the universe, which is the Big Bang theory. The idea of the Big Bang was first put forward by Dr. Edwin Hubble, the man we named the Hubble Space Telescope after. His theory was that at one time all matter was packed into a dense mass at temperatures of many trillions of degrees. Then around 13.8 billion years ago, there was a huge explosion. From that explosion, all of the matter that today forms our planets and stars was born and the universe as we know it was created.

Hubble's idea was confirmed through what has been called the discovery of the past century. On April 24, 1992, the Cosmic Background Explorer satellite, better known as COBE, gave stunning confirmation of the hot Big Bang creation event after investigating the cosmic microwave background radiation of the universe. In many ways, it really was the birth of modern cosmology. And, for many people, the birth of a belief in God.

It is known that something cannot come from nothing. We also know that the universe isn't eternal. Yet, according to the Big Bang theory, something *did* come from nothing. The problem is that you can't just say everything began with the Big Bang and act as if somehow you've explained the origins of the universe, because that still doesn't explain where the matter that exploded came from. In lay terms, where did the stuff that got *banged* come from and who *banged* it? Something (or Someone), somehow, brought that first matter miraculously into existence in such a way that it exploded into the universe. This "something" had to exist outside of space and time, because space and time didn't exist before the Big Bang. Anyone in the scientific community would agree that this could not have happened according to the current laws of physics. Which means we're talking about something *outside* of the laws of physics. Something outside of all natural phenomena.

There's a category for this. If something is outside of natural phenomena, it's called *super*natural, and that puts us in God territory. This really is worth wrestling with. If the universe could not have come into being by itself from nothing (because it is a scientific impossibility that absolute nothingness could produce anything), and if the universe isn't eternal and there really was a creation event through the Big Bang, the questions I raised earlier still remain: Where did the matter that exploded come from and who caused the explosion?

George Smoot, head of the COBE satellite team, who, along with John Mather, won the Nobel Prize in Physics in 2006 for their work on the project, noted that when the COBE satellite measured the ripples in the microwave background radiation that gave confirmation of the Big Bang theory it was "like looking at God."[3] Dr. Robert Jastrow, professor of astronomy at both Columbia University and Dartmouth College, director of the Mount Wilson Institute and manager of the Mount Wilson Observatory, and director of NASA's Goddard Institute for Space Studies for twenty years, made the following comment in regard to the COBE findings: "Now we see how the astronomical evidence leads to a biblical view of the origin of the world."[4] Jastrow went further, saying, "For the scientist who has lived by his faith in the power of reason, the story ends like a bad dream. He has scaled the mountains of ignorance; he is about to conquer the highest peak; as he pulls himself over the final rock, he is greeted by a band of theologians who have been sitting there for centuries."[5]

I know, if you've tracked with me so far, this now begs the question, "Who, then, made God?" We ask this because we live in space and time, and nothing in our understanding of space and time can exist independent of some type of beginning. So if God began our universe, who "began" God? The Christian response is to challenge the presupposition of the question—namely, that God is confined to our understandings of space and time. The Bible points to God as the *Creator* of space and time, independent of their constraints. God is eternal, without beginning or end, and he is not limited to our understandings of beginning or ending.

Now, some may say, "Well, physics just hasn't found the answer to the idea of 'something from nothing' yet. You can't just jump to

God." Perhaps . . . but as Alan Guth, one of the leading physicists of our day at MIT, has written, even if you could come up with a theory that would account for the creation of something from nothing through the laws of physics, you'd still have to account for the *origin* of the laws of physics.

But that's not all there is to think about when it comes to the origins of the universe. Astrophysicists will tell you that what should have happened with the Big Bang was the creation of equal parts matter and antimatter. But that isn't what happened. Particles of matter barely outnumbered particles of antimatter by a rate of about a billion-and-one to a billion. Without that billion-and-one to a billion imbalance between matter and antimatter, all mass in the universe would have self-annihilated, leaving a cosmos made of photons and nothing else. No planets. No stars. Nothing. Which again is what should have happened. Equal parts of matter and antimatter should have been created during the formation of the universe. The universe as we know it should not have come out of the Big Bang. But it did. Something, somehow, stepped in to counter all we know about science and created an imbalance in favor of matter. And no one knows how or why. It was as if there was . . . an intervention.[6]

Design and Order

When it comes to the existence of God, there is more than cause and effect to consider. There are also the issues surrounding design and order. The book of Genesis is the first book of the Bible and contains most of the "origins material." In Genesis we read that at the end of whatever creative process God used to create the universe—and, specifically, our world and all living things within it—there was a single declaration: "It was very good." Meaning, it was good because it was good for the crown of creation: human life. What we're learning from science is how deep and wide that "good" goes, given that everything about the universe, the Milky

Wikimedia Commons

A picture of Earth from NASA

Way, our solar system, and our planet, are perfect for the existence of human life. In other words, what came out of the Big Bang was not chaos, but life-giving, life-sustaining *order*. So much order that it appears to be intricately designed.

How is this accounted for? This is such an obvious question that it has been with us from the most ancient of days, first raised by the Greek philosopher Plato.[7] Here's the thinking: All designs imply a designer. If you find a watch, you understandably assume there is a watchmaker; if you see a building you assume an architect designed it; if you view a painting, you know there was a painter. The greater the complexity of the design and order of something, the more a designer begs to be considered. I once heard it put this way: It's one thing to see a logjam and wonder if there was a beaver behind it; it's another to see Hoover Dam and question whether there was intentionality and purpose behind its creation.

At the time I'm writing this, the Lockheed Martin F-22 Raptor is arguably the top fighter jet in the world.[8] It is super stealthy and virtually invisible to radar. It's an extremely advanced twin-engine aircraft with amazing maneuverability. It can even do something almost unthinkable—a vertical takeoff. Now, imagine you came upon an F-22 in the middle of the desert. You *could* reason that it came together by chance; that the metal was flung together by way of a chaotic sandstorm; that the instruments and panels and wings and advanced technology were all brought together by a freak accident of nature. But it is highly unlikely that this would be your *first* thought. If you came upon an F-22 in the desert, your initial thought would likely be that someone made it and landed it there.

There is staggering design and order to the universe. So much design and order that it seems too much for mere chance. So staggering that it compels many people to consider a "Great Designer" of the universe.

But it goes deeper than that. The anthropic principle, from the Greek word *anthropos* that means "man" or "human," is the idea that our world is uniquely suited to human beings and carbon-based life, the only form of life known to science. But that's putting it mildly. It's *freakishly* suited for human life. There are so many dynamics that if changed only slightly, would make it impossible for us to exist. You can't help but marvel how all of them came together in one planet, in one solar system, in one galaxy, in one universe.

For example, Earth is in what is called a "Goldilocks Zone" around the sun. Remember the Goldilocks story? A little girl, lost in the woods, finds a house where three bears live. She tries some porridge they had left out. One bowl is too hot, one is too cold, but one is just right. That's why scientists call where we live the Goldilocks Zone—the only part of the solar system that's just right for human life. It's not too far and not too close to the home star in order to sustain life. If we were any closer to the sun, all of the oceans would have evaporated. If we were any farther away, they would have frozen.

Then there's the speed of our planet. Our speed enables us to maintain a stable orbit around the sun while never getting too close or too far away. The precision to maintain the right distance at all times while in orbit calls for a very specific speed. So much so that if you were to increase Earth's orbital speed by no more than the square root of two—just 1.4 times its current speed—we would achieve escape velocity. We would fly right out of the solar system if we moved just 1.4 times faster.[9]

And consider how the planet Jupiter, with its mighty gravitational field, redirects the vast majority of comets that would wreak havoc on the inner solar system and, specifically, on Earth. It's as though a mighty shield has been strategically positioned in just the right place to protect our planet.[10] There's also Earth's oxygen-rich atmosphere that not only allows life, but the existence of ozone in the upper atmosphere serving as a shield to protect Earth's surface from most of the sun's molecule-hostile ultraviolet photons.[11] These are just samples of all that has come together on Earth to make life possible.

Even when scientists discover other Earth-like planets, it only adds to the wonder of Earth. "Earth-like" means a planet may have two or three of the twenty-plus elements needed to mimic what we find on Earth. And every Earth-like planet we find falls dramatically short of everything that came together on the planet Earth. For example, when scientists discovered Kepler-22b, just 600 light-years away, it was in the Goldilocks Zone of its solar system. Like Earth, it circled a star similar to the sun at approximately the same distance away from the sun and with a year of 290 days. Yet, it was 2.4 times wider than Earth and covered with water, making it more like the planet Neptune. Size and soil are just two of the twenty-plus elements needed to be like Earth in terms of being suitable for life. Kepler-22b, like every other Earth-like planet we've found, is far from being Earth. Our galaxy contains more than a hundred billion stars. The known universe harbors some hundred billion galaxies. The latest, best estimates suggest there may be as many as 40 billion Earth-like planets in the Milky Way alone. Yet still, in all that vastness, among all those planets, only one can sustain life. And the odds of finding another one are so remote it staggers the imagination, because the odds of everything coming together the way it did on Earth are considered virtually impossible.

But one planet—*super*naturally—did come together.

In a National Public Radio interview, Owen Gingerich, professor of astronomy and the history of science at the Harvard-Smithsonian Center for Astrophysics in Cambridge, noted that "there are so many wonderful details which, if they were changed only slightly, would make it impossible for us to be here, that one just has to feel, somehow, that there is a design in the universe and, therefore, a designer to have worked it out so magnificently."[12] As theoretical physicist Paul Davies of Cambridge has observed, "We are meant to be here."[13] This is such a compelling reality that it causes even the most ardent of atheists to pause. Physicist Stephen Hawking once told a reporter that "the odds against a universe like ours emerging out of something like the Big Bang are enormous. . . . I think clearly there are religious implications."[14] Going even further, Hawking conceded,

> It would be very difficult to explain why the universe should have begun in just this way, except as the act of a God who intended to create beings like us.[15]

About God and Evolution

It was the summer of 1925. The place was the small mountain town of Dayton, Tennessee. The issue at hand was a legal confrontation that made headlines around the world. On one side was William Jennings Bryan and on the other was Clarence Darrow. Their confrontation was not over a crime or misdemeanor; it was not over a legal suit involving a will or a trust. It didn't even involve special prosecutors or a grand jury. In fact, the courts had never encountered a case quite like this one.

The subject was the very origin of human life.

It is known in history books as the "Scopes Trial." A young biology teacher by the name of John T. Scopes was charged with violating a law on the Tennessee books stating you could not teach evolution. As a result, the trial posed defenders of evolutionary theory against those who wanted public schools to teach what was considered to be a biblical view of the origin of the world's inhabitants. William Jennings Bryan represented the state and, by default, those who believed in the biblical view of the creation of human beings. Clarence Darrow represented those who embraced the evolutionary theory.

It really was the clash of two worlds. Bryan was the good-old-boy religious Southerner. Darrow, in favor of evolution, was the outspoken religious agnostic from the North, polished and intellectual, supplied to defend Scopes by the ACLU. Many people do not know that the result of the trial found the teacher guilty, but not before Darrow (the evolutionist) had made a fool of Bryan (the creationist). Bryan allowed himself to be cross-examined by Darrow, arguably the greatest trial lawyer of his day, on the precise accuracy of the Bible. In the course of that examination, Darrow forced Bryan to admit that he couldn't answer even the most basic questions about what the Bible puts forward as truth. Not because there weren't answers, but because Bryan wasn't the sharpest biblical scholar around. So the verdict as it stands in history is intriguing: Bryan won the battle, but he lost the war. While he technically won the case, the conflict stamped the entire debate with an unmistakable image. Evolution vs. creationism came to be seen as the city vs. the country; places like New York

The three main parties of the Scopes Trial—William Jennings Bryan (left), John T. Scopes (center), Clarence Darrow (right)

and Chicago vs. backwoods Dayton, Tennessee; science vs. ignorance; the modern world of the twentieth century vs. the American religious fundamentalism of the nineteenth century. That image has remained firmly in place for nearly a century and so have the lines of debate. Evolution has become the accepted scientific theory of how human beings and all of life developed and came into being. Whether through evolution or not, the biblical idea of a God creating is seen as a view that is antiscientific and out of touch with the real world.[16]

But is that the caricature we should have in mind? A divide between smart and dumb, sophisticated and backward, science and the Bible . . . or even between evolution and creationism? Or is there something more to be considered? Namely, that the real divide is between a *naturalistic* view of the universe (seeing nature as all that there is) and a *theistic* view of the universe (remaining very much open to the existence and activity of God). In other words, a view of the world that sees nothing but the temporal, the material, the natural, over and against a view that is open-minded toward the eternal, the spiritual, yes, even the supernatural. To be sure, those who are Christians believe that God created human beings. If you are a Christian, you are, by necessity, a creationist. You believe that we were wonderfully and carefully designed, and that the entire creative process was miraculously and supernaturally generated and guided by God. So do we now have an insurmountable impasse?

I'm reminded of the joke about a little boy who goes to his dad and asks, "Dad, where did human beings come from?" His father says, "Well, we descended from apes." The little boy then goes to his mother and asks, "Mom, where did human beings come from?" She says, "We were created by God in God's image." The boy says, "But Dad said we descended from apes." "Well," she answers, "I was talking about my side of the family."[17]

But back to the impasse. First, the Bible doesn't say *how* God created, only *that* he created. And it talks about the creation of human beings in a very literary, poetic way using phrases like "from the dust of the earth" and receiving "the breath of life." That doesn't exactly sound like it is trying to be a biology text, does it? Evolution is one of the leading theories in science for the "how" we were created. You may be surprised to hear me say I think this is fine for those who are open to God. You may also be surprised to learn that according to a new study released in February 2019 by the Pew Research Center, this is where most Christians land. The majority of Christians today (as in 58 percent of white evangelical Protestants and 66 percent of black Protestants) "agree that human evolution is real—and that God had a hand in it." Pew acknowledged that perhaps in the past they had been asking the question regarding evolution wrong, meaning not phrasing it in a way to allow both the embrace of evolution along with a role for God.[18] If God used evolution as part of his creative process, so be it. That doesn't mean there wasn't an original Adam and Eve who God breathed an actual soul into at the end of the process to mark the beginning of the human race as we know it, much less a God guiding the entire process. But does the theory of evolution itself point toward a God or away from one?

Let's begin by thinking about the timeline. While the age of the universe is around 13.8 billion years, the age of Earth is about 4.5

Michelangelo's fresco *The Creation of Adam* from the ceiling of the Sistine Chapel, 1512

billion years. But life didn't exist 4.5 billion years ago. It couldn't. That was a geologically violent time; there was constant bombardment from meteorites. Earth itself had to cool and its surface solidify to a crust. Life on Earth, the latest thinking goes, began about 3.8 billion years ago, in the form of single-celled prokaryotic cells, such as bacteria. Multicellular life didn't come into play until more than a billion years later. It's only in the last 570 million years that the kind of life forms we are familiar with even began to evolve, starting with arthropods, followed by fish 530 million years ago, then land plants 470 million years ago, and then forests 385 million years ago. Mammals didn't evolve until just 200 million years ago, and our own species, Homo sapiens, only 200,000 years ago (according to theorists). So humans have been around for a mere 0.004 percent of the earth's history.[19] That's the evolutionary time frame, but also the evolutionary problem.

The whole idea behind naturalistic evolution is that it's a product of time plus chance. But there just hasn't been enough time for Earth to cool and life to be produced naturalistically by chance. Sir

Fred Hoyle, former Plumian Professor of Astronomy and Experimental Philosophy at Cambridge University, determined that if you computed the time required to get all 200,000 amino acids for one human cell to come together by chance, it would be about 293.5 times the estimated age of Earth.[20] Even further, Hoyle, along with his colleague Chandra Wickramasinghe, calculated the odds for all of the functional proteins necessary for a one-cell animal to form in one place by random events. They came up with a figure of one chance in 10 to the 40,000th power—that's the number 1 with 40,000 zeros after it. Since there are only about 10 to the 80th power atoms in the entire universe, Hoyle and Wickramasinghe concluded that this was "an outrageously small probability that could not be faced even if the whole universe consisted of organic soup."[21] For the current proposed evolutionary timeline to work, it would be like having the working dynamics of the latest iPhone along with the entire corporate campus of Apple that produced it to be instantly created—by chance—through a single explosion in a computer geek's garage. If you are going to embrace the theory of evolution, you also need to (seemingly) embrace some kind of outside guiding, enhancing force that sped it along and directed it strategically in the time frame of the age of Earth.

Now, even if you assume there was enough time, or perhaps you want to buy into the theory that mutations and evolutionary leaps can fill all of the time-gaps, you still have the problem of the *initial* complexity of life. (I hope this isn't all too much science. But for some of you, it is precisely science that matters, so on we go.) Darwin himself noted, "If it could be demonstrated that any complex organ existed, which could not possibly have been formed by numerous, successive, slight modifications, my theory would absolutely break down."[22]

Biochemist Michael Behe speaks of Darwin's self-challenge in terms of a mousetrap. The common mousetrap includes a platform, hammer, catch, spring, and holding bar. Each component is required for the mousetrap to function as a mousetrap. You cannot start with a wooden base and catch a few mice, add a bar and catch a few more, and functionally evolve—step by Darwinian step—into the most effective mousetrap, one that has a base, hammer, spring, catch, and holding bar. There must be a minimum number of interacting parts that are assembled to allow the catching of mice before the trap can begin developing into more advanced levels of mice-catching. This is what it means to be *irreducibly complex*: to be a system that consists of several interacting parts that must be in place in order to function as that system. Darwinian evolution depends upon there being a minimal function in place from which the more advanced functions could evolve. But as an irreducibly complex system, our mousetrap could *not* have been produced by continuously improving an initial function of mouse-trapping by slight, successive modifications of the mouse-trapping process. Take away any of the five parts, and no mice would be caught![23] The conclusion is that the mousetrap was somehow made as an intact system. It could not have just evolved into that system. It had to have been designed *as a system* for that purpose.

Yet this is the relatively new and astonishing conclusion of molecular biology: the basic forms of life are *not* simple, but irreducibly complex molecular machines that *cannot* be explained by natural selection working on variation. Think about something like the human eye. According to evolutionary theory, it would have started with a simple, light-sensitive spot, and then evolved to what we see with today. The problem is that when science finally got to the point where we were able to study life at the molecular level, we found it wasn't simple. We found it was irreducibly complex. Which means something, or Someone, had to create those first complex systems from which all of life evolved. Something, or Someone, had to create that first light-sensitive spot. It couldn't have come into existence by itself. You might be able to start simple and get to complex—which is what evolutionary theory maintains—but you can't start complex.[24] Behe, a biochemist, concludes that the result of recent research into life at the molecular level is a loud, piercing cry of intelligent design.[25] There is simply no other explanation for the incredible complexity of the world.

The problem goes deeper than having to explain the complexity that existed at the beginning of the evolutionary process. You also have to consider how the evolutionary process created ever-increasing diversity—in other words, the idea of macroevolution, which is one species evolving into a totally different species. This is very different than microevolution, which is just changes or adaptations within a species. Microevolution is like a dog breeder breeding a dog that sheds less hair. It's still a dog. They can't breed a dog that flies. But that's what naturalistic evolutionary theory—meaning evolution without outside intervention—maintains happened. That microevolution somehow led to macroevolution. That single-cell bacteria led to multicell bacteria, and multicell bacteria led to spiders, and spiders somehow led to fish, and fish somehow led to plants, and plants led to mammals, and it all eventually led to us. How one species creates a completely different species is, at best, vague.

Beyond the lack of time for evolution to have done its work without outside help, beyond tracing the origin of life back to its roots and finding its starting point was so complex that it couldn't have evolved naturally (step by Darwinian step) to get there, *there's the beginning of life itself.* Just like you can't say, "In the beginning, the Big Bang created the heavens and the earth" and consider the questions surrounding the actual origin of the universe solved, you can't say, "Life exists because 3.8 billion years ago it began evolving from single-celled prokaryotic cells." Just like Big Bang theorists have to wrestle with where the stuff that got banged came from and who made it bang, evolutionary theorists have to ask how those first bacteria came to life. It's a profound question: How did life come from non-life? You can say that within chemically rich liquid oceans organic molecules transitioned to self-replicating life, but that's like saying your SUV can become Optimus Prime after it goes through a car wash. It doesn't just happen. Gerd Müller, a highly regarded Austrian evolutionary theorist, gave one of the most honest presentations on this I've heard. As far as I know, he's not a theist much less a Christian. He doesn't argue for God's hand behind the origin of life. But in a lecture as an evolutionary theorist, he confessed that not only does Darwin's theory fail to explain how life originated or explain how complexity developed, it hardly even asks the questions.[26] Yet those are *the* questions.

So what is the leading theory of how this is all solved outside of a God working in and through the process of evolution? This might surprise you, but one of the leading ideas is called *panspermia*— the idea that the first life, along with the beginning complexity, was seeded here from another planet, such as Mars. But that doesn't solve anything. If all the scientific challenges surrounding life beginning on its own on Earth can be solved by saying life began somewhere else and got here on the back of a meteorite, well then how did that life start *there*? So the real decision is not between creationism and evolution, but between theism and naturalism. You can be a theistic evolutionist or a naturalistic evolutionist. It seems to me that the evidence causes being a naturalistic evolutionist the greater leap of faith.

The Humanness of Humans

The last thing I'll put forward that Christians have considered on their way to belief in the existence of God is the "humanness" of humans. Where does human personality come from? It's difficult for many to believe that the human personality—the soul, if you will—evolved naturalistically out of a pool of primordial slime. Legs and arms and lungs, maybe—but what is inside of us? That which makes you, *you*? Consciousness itself? When the philosopher René Descartes attempted to boil down his one and only true starting point for reflection, he came up with his famed phrase *Cogito, ergo sum*. I think, therefore, I am.

But where does that "thinking" come from? How are we able to think, reflect, feel, and reason? There is a voice inside of my head, a personality, a living spirit that I know exists and that is tangible and real when I think to myself. What is that, and where did it come from?

Humans really are different from every other living creature. People who say there's really not much difference between human beings and chimps, because humans are just slightly remodeled chimpanzee-like apes sharing about 99.4 percent of their DNA, lose me. As John Ortberg once noted, "If you really believe that yourself, or if you wonder if that's really true, just ask yourself if you would have a chimpanzee babysit one of your children. Would you date one? Would you hold one morally accountable for its behavior?"[27]

The nature of human identity is not about DNA. There's something else going on, and that includes our spirituality. We are, all of us, deeply spiritual beings regardless of our individual beliefs. One of the most interesting manifestations throughout all civilizations is the deep spiritual hunger of men and women. Anthropologists have discovered that human beings are incurably spiritual and conscious of the idea of God. This was described by Blaise Pascal, the great seventeenth-century philosopher and mathematician, as the "God-shaped hole" in every human being. If there isn't a God, and we evolved naturalistically, that would not make sense.

In reflecting on this, C. S. Lewis noted that drives supposedly come about due to the realities of our world. For example, we have an appetite for food, and there is food to satisfy that need. We have this drive to know God, an authentic spiritual hunger, but there is no God? That doesn't make sense. If it were true, we shouldn't have the drive. Why would creatures who evolved by chance as a result of naturalistic causes alone desire and hunger after a Creator God? Some have suggested that the answer to this is not God at all, but a so-called "God gene" that has been hard-wired into our genetic constitutions. But why would a gene like that have ever evolved?

Wikimedia Commons

The Thinker by Rodin, located at the Musée Rodin in Paris

Some take another tack and say the reason we're so spiritually hungry is simply our desire, our hope for a God. This was the belief of Sigmund Freud, the father of the psychoanalytic school of psychology.[28] The dilemma is that it doesn't explain the universal desire for God throughout time and across civilization. At some point, particularly in our modern context, you would think that the wish, desire, or need for God would simply end. Yet it only grows, which makes no evolutionary sense if there is no God.

Coupled with this is our inner sense of morality. According to a major study by Oxford University, everyone everywhere shares seven universal moral rules. In fact, all societies are held together by these seven rules. The huge study of sixty different cultures around the world found that all communities operate under these seven basic moral codes. "It was the largest and most comprehensive and widespread survey of morals ever conducted, and aimed to find out whether different societies had different versions of morality."

The study found they did not. Here is what we all share in common—across continents, religions, and politics—and value as important:

1. Help your family.
2. Help your group.
3. Return favors.

4. Be brave.

5. Defer to superiors.

6. Divide resources fairly.

7. Respect the property of others.

The study also found that inherent within this code was caring for frail relatives, passing on property to offspring, going to war if needed to protect the group, and respecting elders.[29]

Intuitively, each of us appeals to some sense of right and wrong in our dealings with ourselves, with others, and with the world. If we have to get up from our seat for a moment in a crowded venue and someone sits in our place, we naturally say, "Hey, that's my seat! I was there first!" When we do that, we are appealing to some behavioral standard that the other person is supposed to know and accept. And there is a surprising consensus from civilization to civilization, culture to culture, as to what is right and what is wrong. When you take the time to study the moral teaching of the ancient Egyptians, Babylonians, Hindus, Chinese, Greeks, and Romans, it is amazing how similar they are to each other morally. For example, selfishness is never admired and loyalty is always praised. Men may have differed as to whether you should have one wife or fourteen, but they have always agreed that you must not simply have any woman you like.[30] As C. S. Lewis once observed: "My argument against God was that the universe seemed so cruel and unjust. But how had I got this idea of *just* and *unjust*? A man does not call a line crooked unless he has some idea of a straight line."[31] Somehow it seems we have an innate sense of right and wrong. Or, as Darwin once replied when asked whether man was in any way unique from other life forms, "Man is the only animal that blushes."[32] Where does this come from independent of an outside source?

National Public Radio did a story on the most challenging questions facing science based on an article in *The Guardian*, one of the biggest news publications in the UK.[33] And what were those questions plaguing scientific minds? The very ones we've detailed in this chapter. For example, "How did life come about?" Translation: "How did life come from non-life? How did something *dead* become *alive*? If everything was once dead, how did life appear?" There are no scientific answers.

Another question: "What makes us human?" From the NPR story: "We have three times more neurons than a gorilla, but our DNAs are almost identical. Many animals have a rudimentary language, can use tools and recognize themselves in mirrors. So, what is it that differentiates us from them?"

Then the question, "What is consciousness?" Meaning: "How is it that the brain generates the self of self, the unique experience that we have of being . . . unique? Can the brain be reverse-engineered to be modeled by machines? Or is this a losing proposition? And why is there a consciousness at all?"

Again, no scientific answers.

But there are theological ones. In the beginning, there was a God who created and, through that creation, sent out a compelling message about his existence: that he does, indeed, exist.

Such considerations are turning more than Christian heads, as was the case for atheist Antony Flew shortly before his death. Flew was the famed Oxford philosophy professor who wrote the quintessential articles in favor of atheism for college philosophy textbooks the world over. But before his death, he renounced his atheism. Why? Cause and effect, design and order, the challenges to a purely naturalistic view of evolution, and the humanness of humans. He's not alone. Some of the greatest names in science will tell you that they have not only become believers in God but card-carrying Christians. Not *despite* science, but *because* of it. People like Francis Collins, who led the Human Genome Project that produced the first reference sequence of the human DNA instruction book, and who became the director of the National Institutes of Health. He looked at everything science has discovered about the beginnings of the universe and the beginnings of life, and determined it was "God's elegant plan for creating humankind," all complementary to his faith in Christ.[34]

The "Hiddenness" of God

Of course, after such a lengthy conversation about things that point to God it would be reasonable to ask why God isn't more direct with his existence. The short answer is because whatever relationship he may have with you, he wants it to be real—not forced or coerced. Imagine God making himself known to you in the most unmistakable of ways (and, to be sure, he could). Would your belief in him be anything other than something imposed upon you? C. S. Lewis weighed in on this in an even more telling manner:

> God will invade. But I wonder whether people who ask God to interfere openly and directly in our world quite realise what it will be like when He does. When that happens, it is the end of the world. When the author walks on to the stage the play is over. . . . For this time it will be God without disguise; something so overwhelming that it will strike either irresistible love or irresistible horror into every creature. It will be too late then to choose your side. There is no use saying you choose to lie down when it has become impossible to stand up. That will not be the time for choosing; it will be the time when we discover which side we really have chosen, whether we realised it before or not.[35]

And the longer answer to those who ask, "Why doesn't God make himself known? Why doesn't he reveal himself more clearly?" is that Christians believe he has.

But we'll get to Jesus in a bit.

It's Your Choice

In the 1850s, the German philosopher Friedrich Nietzsche proclaimed "God is dead." During the 1960s, someone took Nietzsche's famous slogan and wrote it in spray paint on a billboard near Union Seminary in New York: "God is dead—Nietzsche." Then someone else, undoubtedly a seminary student, took a can of spray paint and wrote: "Nietzsche is dead—God." The debate is hardly academic. More consequence for thought and action flow from the question "Does God exist?" than almost any other question you can raise. The only question that can match its significance is built on it: "If God exists, what is he like?"

The Christian answer might surprise you.

2

BUT WHAT KIND OF GOD?

"What is . . . God?"
I asked the earth and it answered:
"I am not He";
and all things that are in the earth
made the same confession.

Augustine, *Confessions*, Book X

I once heard of a little girl who was drawing a picture at school. Her teacher came over and asked her what she was drawing.

"I'm drawing a picture of God."

Her teacher said, "Honey, you know, nobody really knows what God looks like."

And the little girl said, "Well, they will when I get through!"

Whether you accept or reject the existence of God, most of us have a picture of that God that we have drawn in our minds, usually based on a series of ideas, feelings, and past experiences from our life. Christianity presents a picture of God that is both unique and compelling, but it may be a picture that is very different from the one you've drawn, even if you think you've been drawing the Christian one. George Buttrick, former chaplain at Harvard, recalled how students would come into his office and say, "I don't believe in God." Buttrick would then reply, "Sit down and tell me what kind of God you don't believe in. I probably don't believe in that God either."[1]

Now, there's a lot the Christian faith holds about the Person of God: God is Spirit, not flesh and blood; God is personal, not an impersonal energy force; God is living, not a dead totem; God is infinite in terms of space, time, knowledge, and power; God is constant, not in a state of flux. For many people, the real question is not about the Person of God, but his nature. Is this God moral? Does he have integrity? Is he loving? Many aren't so sure. In fact, most people who reject the idea of God don't reject the possibility of his existence—they reject what they think they know about him. Particularly, what they think they know about him from the Bible. The reason for this is simple. Sometimes it can seem like the God of the Bible acts in ways we would never dream of acting ourselves. This makes it hard to believe *that* God—or what we think we know about that God—is *right*. Many people feel the God of the Bible is angry, mean, capricious, and a bit too quick to send people to hell. They don't even like the idea of a God who would create a hell, much less send people there. And if he's supposed to be so good and loving, then why is there so much suffering in the world and why has it gone on for so long? Why doesn't God step in and stop it? To a lot of people, it seems like we need a better God than the one that we have—or at least a better God than the God of the Bible. I've heard people say in one way or another, "When I look at the world and how it's being run, how it's playing out . . . if I was God, I could do better." As an atheist blogger once put it (in a post that has since been taken down), "If I was God, the following words and phrases would not exist . . .

| War | Drugs | Disease |
| Hunger | Murder | Poverty |

Rape	Oppression	Sorrow
Poor	Victim	Kill
Fight	Gun	Sadness
Genocide	Third World	Loneliness
Famine	Accident	Death
Jealousy	Weapon	Anger
Slavery	Atrocity	Apology
Homeless	Bomb	Old
Conflict	Abortion	Need
Hate	Molestation	Evil
Natural Disaster	Dictator	Sick
Greed	Steal	Cancer
Crime	Mental Illness	Hell"[2]

On Evil and Suffering

One of the most chilling places I have ever visited is the Dachau Concentration Camp just outside of Munich, Germany. It opened on March 22, 1933. It was the first of the German concentration camps, and the only one kept open throughout the Nazi era. It became a model for every other concentration camp—camps with names such as Auschwitz, Buchenwald, Bergen-Belsen, and Ravensbruck. Dachau did not close until liberated by American troops on April 29, 1945, so it had a twelve-year nightmarish run. By the end of its operation, more than 200,000 human beings from across Europe were robbed of their freedom, tortured, exploited, and—for tens of thousands—eventually killed on its grounds.

I recall finding myself in a part of the camp that was somewhat off the beaten path. I wandered over to a ditch and there was a placard hidden among the weeds that said the man-made ditch served as a stream to carry away the blood from all the people who were shot in the head. It is hard to even explain the emotion

The gate at the entrance of the Dachau Concentration Camp with the phrase *Arbeit Macht Frei* ("Work will set you free")

of seeing that and reading that sign unless you were standing there.

The most spiritually persistent question people ask—across every world religion, every philosophy, every worldview—is, "Why is there evil and suffering in the world?" It's the question that lingers and never goes away, and it's the most troubling question for people spiritually, crying out to be answered. People cannot seem to wrap their heads around why evil and suffering exist in the world, and when this question is not answered it can become a huge stumbling block. This is not a question that the Christian faith alone must answer. If you reject Christianity because of the existence of suffering in the world, then you need to reject every philosophy, every worldview, every ideology, every religion. Because the reality of suffering is not just unique for Christianity to explain. I don't care if you're Buddhist, Muslim, Mormon, Scientologist, Hindu, or nothing at all—everyone must answer the question about why this is such a screwed-up world. Even atheists. It's actually one of the biggest arguments *against* atheism. Atheists may not believe in God, but they believe in the inherent goodness of human beings and the inevitable upward progression of naturalistic evolution. Which means that human beings should be becoming increasingly good and noble, peaceful and humane, through the advances of education, politics, and technology. So in theory it should be a better world every day.

It's not.

But there is a reason this question about evil and suffering is often laid solely at the feet of Christians. The Bible teaches that God is all-powerful, able to do anything he wants. Further, the Bible teaches that God is thoroughly good—not mean, capricious, or vindictive. Yet bad things happen. There is suffering in the world. And for many, many people, those dynamics just don't mix. If God is good and all-powerful, he shouldn't allow bad things to happen. Since they *do* happen, people then decide either God isn't good or he isn't all-powerful. Rabbi Harold Kushner, in his book *When Bad Things Happen to Good People*, embraced the idea that God cares but is powerless to do anything about it. Elie Wiesel, who suffered through the Holocaust, said of the God described by Kushner, "If that's who God is, why doesn't He resign and let someone more competent take his place?"[3] This was the sentiment of C. S. Lewis who, after his wife died from cancer, wrote: "Not that I am (I think) in much danger of ceasing to believe in God. The real danger is of coming to believe such dreadful things about Him. The conclusion I dread is not, 'So there's no God after all,' but 'So this is what God's really like. Deceive yourself no longer.'"[4]

So let me try to give the answer the Christian faith gives to the question of suffering. You can compare it to any other answer you want. And it's really more of a story than some sterile, textbook answer. A deeply relational story. But before I tell it, let me state the obvious: there is no answer that can be given that will satisfy the emotional pain of suffering. In the movie *Shadowlands*, Anthony Hopkins portrays C. S. Lewis, whose wife died soon after their marriage. In the movie, a minister tries to give Lewis a "God knows best" pat answer, causing Lewis to explode: "No! This is a mess. That's all anyone can say—it's just a mess!" For most of us, though, the search is not for an answer that will alleviate the pain as much as a reason for *why* the pain was ever allowed. So let me see if I can tell you that story.

In the Beginning

God made us in order to love us. We are tenderly crafted and de-signed, each as an individual, for the purpose of being related to, known, and deeply cherished. Yet this means we are also given the freedom to make choices with our life, to live as fully conscious, self-determining beings. Even to the point of whether we choose to respond to the Creator's love. God did not choose to seduce us against our will. Instead, he determined to woo us, knowing that in so doing, we might very well spurn his love. But this is the only way to have the relationship *be* a relationship.

This is the dynamic at the heart of human existence. God could have *made* me love him, but if he had, his relationship with me—and mine with him—would be meaningless. God wants my rela-tionship with him and with others to be real. So when he created me, he had to take the risk of setting me free. The great leader of Israel, Joshua, voiced some of the most famous words in Scripture when speaking of this amazing liberty in relation to his own life: "If serving the LORD seems undesirable to you, then choose for yourselves this day whom you will serve. . . . But as for me and my household, we will serve the LORD" (Josh. 24:15).

The first instance of this freedom to choose love was, as you might expect, made by the first humans, Adam and Eve. They were given one and only one instruction: "Don't eat from this one tree." The tree in the middle of the garden stood as the great authenticator that the love between the first humans and God was

Photo of *Adam and Eve* by Raphael (1509–11), ceiling panel at the Apostolic Palace

real. Then they chose to eat the fruit from that tree. They made the conscious, purposeful decision to go against the love, against the relationship. The Lover was spurned.

And then all hell broke loose.

The decision the first humans made to reject God's leadership and ongoing intimacy within a relationship with him radically altered God's original design for how the world would operate and how life would be lived. Theologians have termed this *the fall*, and talk about how we now live in a fallen world. We live in a world that is not the way God intended it to be. When Satan told Eve that if she ate the fruit from the tree God had forbidden them to eat from that she would not die, he lied. That became the day death and dying were born into the human race. Their choice forever stained the relationship of loving intimacy that had been intended for eternity within the Lover's heart.

Langdon Gilkey observes that few of us find it easy to believe that one act of disobedience brought about a fall for the whole human race that is now continued in us by inheritance. Yet reflecting on his experience in a Japanese internment camp during World War II, where prisoners representing a cross-section of humanity were forced to participate in a living laboratory of community, Gilkey noted that the theological idea of a pervasive warping of our wills is the most accurate description of the reality of life. "What the doctrine of sin has said about man's present state," Gilkey concluded, "seemed to fit the facts as I found them."[5]

As it does for most.

In a scene from the movie *Grand Canyon*, an attorney tries to get around a traffic jam, but he gets lost in a series of back streets that take him farther and farther into parts of the town that are anything but the tony suburbs of his world. His expensive car stalls, and he uses his cell phone to call for a tow truck. While he waits, five young street toughs come up and circle his car and begin to threaten him. The tow truck arrives, and the driver begins to hook up the car, ignoring the five young men trying to steal it. They, in turn, threaten him. He then takes the leader aside and says, "Man, the world ain't supposed to work like this. Maybe you don't know that, but this ain't the way it's supposed to be. I'm supposed to be able to do my job without askin' you if I can. And that dude is supposed to be able to wait with his car without you rippin' him off. Everything's supposed to be different than what it is here."[6]

He is right.

50

And the results of our collective choice to turn away from God run so deep that it isn't just moral sin and evil that we face, but natural evil as well. The whole world is sick. In the Bible, we're told that "the whole creation has been groaning" (Rom. 8:22). This is why we have earthquakes and tidal waves, volcanoes and mudslides, wildfires and birth defects, famine and AIDS. Our world is "The Groaning Planet," writes Philip Yancey, an author who has invested much of his life in exploring issues like these. The pain and suffering and heartache is a huge cosmic "scream . . . that something is wrong . . . that the entire human condition is out of whack."[7] These are far from original insights, much less contemporary ones. The medieval Christian philosopher Boethius aptly noted that "evil is not so much an infliction as a deep set infection."[8] This raises a provocative point: God is not behind what is tragic with this world, much less responsible for it—people are. Or, as G. K. Chesterton once wrote to the editor in response to a request by the London *Times* for an essay on the topic, "What's Wrong with the World,"

> Dear Sir:
>   In response to your article, "What's wrong with the world"—I am.
>
>   Yours truly,
>   G. K. Chesterton[9]

Yancey, whom I mentioned earlier, was contacted by a television producer after the death of Princess Diana and asked to appear on a show to explain how God could have possibly allowed such a tragic accident. "Could it have had something to do with a drunk driver going 90 miles per hour in a narrow tunnel?" he asked the producer. "How, exactly, was God involved?" From this, Yancey reflected on the pervasive nature of the mindset that *our* actions are actually an indictment of *God*. For example, when boxer Ray "Boom Boom" Mancini killed a Korean boxer in a match, the athlete said in a press conference, "Sometimes I wonder why God does the things He does." Or when, in a letter to a Christian family therapist, a young woman wrote how she became pregnant while dating a man and wanted to know why God allowed that to happen to her. Or when South Carolina mother Susan Smith gave her official confession to pushing her two sons into a lake to drown, she said that as she released the car she then went running after it as it sped down the ramp, screaming: "Oh God! Oh God, no! . . . Why did you let this happen!"

Yancey raises the decisive question by asking, "Exactly what role did God play in a boxer pummeling his opponent, a teenage couple losing control in a backseat, or a mother drowning her children?"[10] God let us choose; we did, and our choices have brought continual pain and heartache and destruction. Our self-destructive bent seems to know no bounds. As historian Will Durant once wryly observed, "In the last 3,421 years of recorded history only 268 have seen no war."[11] On a more personal level, here's how one psychologist described it: "We drink too much, or gamble compulsively, or allow pornography to control our minds. We drive too fast and work like there's no tomorrow. We challenge the boss disrespectfully and then blow up when he strikes back. We spend money we don't have and can't possibly repay. We fuss and fight at home and create misery. . . . We toy with the dragon of infidelity. . . . Then when the 'wages' of those sins and foolishness come due, we turn our shocked faces up to heaven and cry, 'Why me, Lord?' In truth, we are suffering the natural consequences of dangerous behavior that is guaranteed to produce pain."[12]

Returning to the Dachau story: when my wife and I went to visit, we took a taxi from our hotel in Munich. We told our German driver where we wanted to go. He didn't say anything for a long time; he just drove. Then, out of the blue, he said in his thick German accent, "Where you go, it is a very painful place." Then he paused again and said, "When I was ten or eleven years old, my teacher took us here. She said, 'We were responsible for two world wars—now we are responsible for freedom.'" Then he paused again and said, "Those were the right words to say, I think."

And I think so too.

A Father's Love

After reading all of that you may be tempted to say, "Well, if he knew how it was going to turn out, he should have never created us!" because everything from cancer to concentration camps doesn't seem worth it. Yet when we blithely say such things, we betray how little we know of true love. Yes, God took a risk. Yes, the choice he gave each of us has resulted in pain and heartache and even tragedy. Yes, it would be tempting to say that it would have been easier on everyone—including God—never to have endured it. But that's not the way love—real love, at least—works. To remember this, I need only reflect on one of the most defining realities of my life—my own role as a father. I have four children, all of whom are now grown with children of their own. I remember the season of parenting when I had to let go of each one. Seeing them get married, move to other cities, start their own lives and families. Each became free in ways they had never been free before to leave, to make choices on their own, and even to turn away from us if they so wished.

It wasn't easy. Rebecca, my oldest, was obviously the first child I had to go through this with. I thought it was hard when she went off to her first birthday party and the birthday girl suddenly announced at the start of a game, "Everyone can play but Rebecca," sending her home in tears.

I thought taking her to first grade, walking her to her desk, and then turning to leave her for an entire day for the first time—and then hearing how another child had purposefully tripped her on the playground—was hard.

I thought pulling out splinters or holding her through the night when she had a fever was hard.

I thought watching her experience the onset of puberty and the painful awkwardness and insecurity of becoming a teenager was hard.

I thought it was hard to send her off to college, where she could go her own way like never before, make her own decisions, choose her own paths and, in the process, wound and be wounded in ways that were unthinkable when I first held her in my arms.

But walking her down an aisle and putting her hand—the hand I had always held from the day she was born—into the hands of someone else . . .

Now *that* was hard.

Each stage involved granting love-filled freedom. But now our relationship is just that—a relationship, like never before. Without guarantees, without ties, without obligations. It can be scary. She calls, or she doesn't. She texts, or she doesn't. She visits, or she doesn't. It's a relationship. But as her father, as the one who loves her more than anyone, who would lay down his life for her instantly, let me tell you what has *never* entered my mind.

Never having her.

Never bringing her into the world.

Never going through life with her.

Even though she can reject me, hurt me, turn from me, and tear out my heart by hurting herself as well as others. If someone were to say, "Why did you ever bother?" my only reply would be, "You have obviously never been a father." And as one who has stood by the side of countless other fathers who have endured far more pain and anguish than I have—suffering through prodigal years, chronic illnesses, and even death—I can attest to the solidarity that is held toward the sentiment. No matter the wound, no matter the cost, the worth and value of bringing our children into the world goes without question.

God's desire to be in a relationship with us is why suffering cannot be reduced to mere injustice, much less punishment. As a *Time* magazine reporter attempting to understand Christianity's unique perspective rightly noted, "It is a harrowing invitation to a higher dialogue."[13] That higher dialogue is love. When one loves, there is risk—risk of suffering, risk of loss, risk of rejection. But without this willingness to be wounded on the deepest of levels, there cannot exist authentic relationship on the deepest of levels. God's great longing is to commune with us for eternity. As C. S. Lewis wrote in *The Problem of Pain*, "Try to exclude the possibility of suffering which the order of nature and the existence of free-wills involves, and you will find that you have excluded life itself."[14] God has refused to let the perils of authentic love prevent him from loving. As Lewis writes in *The Four Loves*,

> To love at all is to be vulnerable. Love anything, and your heart will certainly be wrung and possibly be broken. If you want to make sure of keeping it intact, you must give your heart to no one, not even to an animal. Wrap it carefully round with hobbies and little luxuries; avoid all entanglements; lock it up safe in the casket or coffin of your selfishness. But in that casket—safe, dark, motionless, airless—it will change. It will not be broken; it will become unbreakable, impenetrable, irredeemable. . . . The only place outside Heaven where you can be perfectly safe from all the dangers . . . of love is Hell.[15]

Hopefully now you can imagine why God chose to risk creating us out of a Father's love for us, but what would our choice have been? Apart from rare and tragic cases of suicide, where emotional and psychological trauma drive a person to self-destruction, few truly wish for their lives to end. Glib statements such as "I wish I had never been born" are seldom meant. Even among the most wretched of conditions, we intuitively understand the priceless nature of life itself, clinging to it tenaciously and thanking God for every next breath. Which is why it's equally glib to say, "Why doesn't God just end it all now?" If God wiped out all evil, all wrongdoing, every person who committed harm against another, tonight, how many of us would live to see the dawn? I know I wouldn't. You see, God *could* wipe out all evil, all suffering, this very night. But he doesn't, and the reason he doesn't is because of his love for people like you and me. Because if at midnight tonight God decreed that all evil would be stamped out in the universe, not one of us would be here at 12:01.

So Where Is God?

So where is God when it comes to the potential pain in my daughter's life—the pain that might come her way and the pain that might flow back to me—because I chose to have her? The same place God is when it comes to *all* of the pain in this world: right by our side, caring for us, weeping with us, and longing to hold us in his arms.

Philip Yancey once wrote about a pastor friend of his who was in conflict with his fifteen-year-old daughter. He knew she was using birth control, and several nights she had not bothered to come home at all. As parents, he and his wife had tried various forms of punishment, but nothing seemed to make much of a difference. Their daughter lied to them, deceived them, and always found a way to turn the tables on them, blaming her behavior on them for being so strict. Yancey's friend said that he remembered standing in front of the window in his living room one night, staring out into the darkness and waiting for his daughter to come home. He said he felt such rage. He was so angry with his daughter for the way she manipulated him and his wife and constantly tried to find ways to hurt them. He was also upset because he knew she was hurting herself more than anyone. In that moment he understood more than ever before the passages in the Bible where God expressed frustration—passages talking about how the people knew how to wound God and how God would cry out in pain.

"And yet I must tell you," he said, "when my daughter came home that night (or rather the next morning), I wanted nothing in the world so much as to take her in my arms, to love her, to tell her I wanted the best for her. I was a helpless, lovesick father." Yancey writes that now, when he reflects on God, he holds up that image of the lovesick father. Because it really is the most biblical image you can have—a God who is standing in front of the window, gazing achingly into the darkness, waiting for his child to come home.[16]

Countless numbers of people who have opened up their heart to God's presence and comfort in the midst of their pain have found this to be true. After being a prisoner in Ravensbruck, one of the infamous concentration camps of Nazi Germany, Corrie ten Boom traveled throughout the world, telling her story of suffering in the context of a faith in God. For thirty-three years following her time in Ravensbruck, she never had a permanent home. When she was eighty-five years old, some friends provided her with a lovely home in California. It was a luxury she never dreamed she would have. One day, as a friend was leaving her home after a visit, he said, "Corrie, hasn't God been good to give you this beautiful place?" She replied firmly, "God was good when I was in Ravensbruck, too."[17]

One of the most difficult tasks I was ever called upon to perform was as a pastor of a church outside of Louisville, Kentucky, during my seminary years. A friend and member of the church called and told me that his next-door neighbor had just committed suicide. She was the mother of five girls, and her youngest daughter had found her. They had no church, no pastor. He asked them if it would be all right if he called someone from his church to come. They said yes, so he called me. When I arrived, I saw huddled in a corner of the house the five daughters with their father. I thought: *What am I doing here? What could I possibly say, what could I ever do, that would help at this moment?* I went over to the family, introduced myself, and said the only words I could think of: "I just want you to know that I'm sorry. I'm so very, very sorry."

The girl who had found her mother looked up at me and said, "Would you pray for us?" So I prayed. I don't remember a single word of that prayer. But when I finished, that little girl looked up at me and simply said, "God's here, isn't he?"

And I said, "Yes, he is."

She said, "I thought so. I could feel him hugging me when you prayed. It's going to be all right, isn't it?"

And I said, "Yes, honey, it's going to be hard, but it's going to be all right."

But being with us is not all that God has done.

He's invested himself in the process of healing the wounds that come from our choices by entering into the suffering process *with* us in order to lift us *out* of it. The heart of the Christian faith is that God himself in human form came to earth in the person of Jesus and *suffered*. He *knows* about pain. He *knows* about rejection. He *knows* about hunger, injustice, and cruelty because he has *experienced* suffering. An ancient graffito found at the museum on the Palatine Hill in Rome, Italy, shows a crucified figure with a donkey's head, bearing the inscription "Alexamenos worships his god." While meant to disparage and even mock, the image rings true.

We worship, as German theologian Jurgen Moltmann observed, the *crucified* God. Jesus on the cross was God entering into the reality of human suffering, experiencing it just like we do, in order to demonstrate that even when we used our free will to reject him, his love never ended. This was not suffering for its own sake, but suffering so that we might use our free will to choose again— this time, making the *right* choice. Frederick Buechner put it this way: "Like a father saying about his sick child, 'I'd do anything to make you well,' God finally calls his own bluff and does it."[18] The ultimate deliverance, the most significant healing, the most strategic rescue, has come. Our greatest and most terrible affliction has been addressed. God has given us the greatest answer to our questions. He has given us himself.

And he is going to keep giving himself to any and all who will turn to him until the end of time. And time will come to an

"Alexamenos worships his god" is a second-century pagan graffito depicting a crucified figure with a donkey's head.

end. A missionary was once asked what Jesus will say when he returns to the earth, because Jesus himself said he would return at the end of all things. He thought it was an odd question, but then he remembered a verse in the Bible about Jesus's return from the first letter that the apostle Paul wrote to the people of the church in Thessolonica. It says, "For the Lord himself will come down from heaven *with a commanding shout*" (1 Thess. 4:16 NLT, emphasis added). The person wanted to know what Jesus will shout. The missionary thought a moment, and then it came to him. He said, "Enough." Jesus will shout, "Enough!" Enough suffering, enough starvation, enough terror. Enough death, enough indignity, enough lives trapped in hopelessness. Enough sickness and disease. At the end, when he returns, "Christ will shout, 'Enough!'"[19]

That is the story you need to know.

This raises the real question when it comes to our broken world: Will pain and suffering drive you *away* from God, or will it drive you *to* God? The whole reason it is being allowed and that "Enough!" has not been shouted yet is because God is hoping for people like you to turn to him. You may say, "You mean

God endures all that for . . . me?" Yes. Do you want to know the reason?

He's your Father.

The God of the Bible

The questions about why the world is such a sin-stained, screwed-up place are not the end of the matter, are they? While every faith, every philosophy, every worldview must speak to the reason for the existence of a very broken world, the Christian faith has another set of questions waiting in the wings. These questions have to deal with the fact that when people go to the Bible to learn more about God, they find out that it's God who seems to be behind a lot of the pain and suffering—even the one causing it! It's the God of the Bible doling out capital punishment for seemingly minor infractions; the one who is asking for blood sacrifices; the one who is calling for the slaughter of entire people groups. The late Christopher Hitchens wrote a book on this titled *God Is Not Great*. Fellow sympathizer Richard Dawkins calls the God of the Bible a "moral monster." It doesn't take familiarity with the names and places to feel the force of Dawkins's ruthless examination of, particularly, the Old Testament text of the Bible. For example, Dawkins calls God's commanding Abraham to sacrifice his son Isaac to be "disgraceful" and tantamount to "child abuse and bullying." He calls the killing of the Canaanites by the Israelites, as a dictate from God, an "ethnic cleansing" in which "bloodthirsty massacres" were carried out with "xenophobic relish." He says that the Israelite leader Joshua's destruction of Jericho is "morally indistinguishable from Hitler's invasion of Poland, or Saddam Hussein's massacres of the Kurds." Conclusion? "The God of the Old Testament is arguably the most unpleasant character in all fiction; jealous and proud of it; a petty, unjust, unforgiving control-freak; a vindictive, bloodthirsty ethnic cleanser; a misogynistic, homophobic, racist, infanticidal, genocidal, filicidal, pestilential, megalomaniacal, sadomasochistic, capriciously malevolent bully."[20]

So is the God of the Bible a moral monster?

When you read the Bible and find instances of seemingly harsh punishment, the call for sacrifices and even the mass slaughter of entire nations—which, I might add, you do find—do we still have a good and loving God on our hands? Or do we have a terribly evil Being to be rejected, and certainly not to be believed in?

There's no doubt you can paint a picture of the God of the Bible any way you want if you are selective in what you focus on and take the Scripture out of its original context and meaning. I once saw a YouTube video titled "Scary Mary." It was a collection of scenes from Disney's classic family film *Mary Poppins*. The mashup took what looked like "scary" scenes from the movie out of context, changed the background music, and produced a trailer as though it was a horror film. The mashup obviously did not reveal the true character of Mary Poppins. It was creative but misleading, showing Mary Poppins as evil. Could we be doing this with our image of the God of the Bible?

Slaughters

Let's look at just one of the concerns about the God of the Bible, arguably the one most discussed—the slaughter of the Canaanites. It is what some have called the most difficult and bloody part of the Bible, and the one that on the surface is the most ethically troubling. It's found in the Old Testament book of Deuteronomy. The context is critical. God led the people of Israel out of slavery and out of Egypt. He was not only forming them into a new people, a new nation, but taking them to a new land that would become known as the Promised Land. But it wasn't just given to them. They had to take it, possess it, and, at times, conquer it. And that's what brings us to one of the bloodiest scenes in the Bible: the slaughter of the Canaanites by the Israelites on the directive of God himself. There are several places where this is referenced in the Bible. Here's an overview description:

> As you approach a town to attack it, you must first offer its people terms for peace. If they accept your terms and open the gates to you, then all the people inside will serve you in forced labor. But if they refuse to make peace and prepare to fight, you must attack the town. When the LORD your God hands the town over to you, use your swords to kill every man in the town. But you may keep for yourselves all the women, children, livestock, and other plunder. You may enjoy the plunder from your enemies that the LORD your God has given you. (Deut. 20:10–14 NLT)

(Before you read on, let me just add that this was *not* a license to rape and pillage. It was later detailed that if an Israelite took one of these women, it meant that they were going to have to take them as their wife and treat them with all the respect and decorum that came with that marriage. Now let's continue reading.)

> But these instructions apply only to distant towns, not to the towns of the nations in the land you will enter. In those towns that the LORD your God is giving you as a special possession, destroy every living thing. You must completely destroy the Hittites, Amorites, Canaanites, Perizzites, Hivites and Jebusites, just as the LORD your God has commanded you. This will prevent the people of the land from teaching you to imitate their detestable customs in the worship of their gods, which would cause you to sin deeply against the LORD your God. (Deut. 20:15–18 NLT)

So was that an indiscriminate massacre, an ethnic cleansing along the lines of Hitler and the Jewish Holocaust, or Saddam Hussein's slaughter of the Kurds? Something that deserves not only universal condemnation, but a complete rejection of the God of the Bible? Or is there something more here?

First, this was more than just an invasion or conquest. This was God's planned punishment of the people of Canaan for their ways, long in the making and in the coming. Yes, God was displacing them from the land to give it to the people of Israel. But that displacement came because of their ferocious, habitual, unrepentant wickedness. And I do mean wicked. The Canaanites were marked by the worst possible aspects of slavery, religious prostitution, and sexual cults. (Not that there's anything good about slavery, but think taking slavery to the darkest place that you can possibly take it.) Scholars have called the Canaanite cult religion the most sexually depraved of any in the ancient world.[21] They had given themselves over to every kind of sexual depravity, including incest and even bestiality. At their worst, their orgiastic worship of idols even included human sacrifice—both of children and adults. There's imagery of their cult sexual practice of bathing themselves in blood.

The Bible says that God had been tolerating this for more than four hundred years. Their wickedness kept increasing and increasing and God kept enduring it. Four hundred years of restraint and patience. Why? Because no matter what you've heard, judgment is always his last resort. But the wickedness reached a point where Scripture talks about how God couldn't stomach it anymore and he vomited them out of his mouth (see Gen. 15:16 and Lev. 18:24–30). So what stands out in the Bible is not God's acts of justice, but how much he is marked by mercy. By restraint. But this was a time when God determined that there was no other recourse but divine judgment.

A second point to remember is that this was a divine, God-ordained action. In other words, it was God's call to make. Not just the punishment, but the possession of the land—who he was going to give that land to. Israel didn't have an inherent right to the land. Neither did the Canaanites. But God did. He could give it to whomever he wanted. So if someone says, "I can't believe God kicked the Canaanites out and gave away their land," an appropriate response is, "What do you mean by 'their land'?" This was God's land. He made it. He could do with it whatever he wanted to do. Israel would never have been justified in doing this had God not ordered it. But God did. So don't think about this as a simple invasion of one nation into another. Or a strong army beating a weaker army, as if strength or desire gives anyone the right to be aggressive. You'll never find that in the Bible. This was God saying, "I'm telling you, this land is now yours. It is not theirs."

But there's a third observation to make here, and it's about the command to "destroy every living thing" in the cities. When you read something like that it sounds over the top and unnecessary even for divine judgment. But the command was for the cities, not the outlying areas. This is a critical point. In the culture of the ancient Near East, most people lived in outlying areas, not the cities. The cities were military fortifications for soldiers and military officers.[22] It's not where the women and children, farmers and laborers lived. So in terms of warfare, this was not about targeting civilians. Also, in the ancient language of the day, even the phrase about destroying everyone in the city was common hyperbole. It wasn't about literally taking every life, but ensuring that the war was won, the enemy defeated, the task accomplished. Think how in our day we talk about a sports team that blew their opponent away, or slaughtered them, or annihilated them. It's a form of rhetoric. When you study the language of the ancient Near Eastern cultures, this was very common. They would talk about how they destroyed every man, and then later talk about what they were going to do with the survivors. In other words, destroying everything meant winning decisively, not literally destroying everything. This was more about purifying than purging.

Which brings up the final point to remember in all this, one that is unavoidable: it's the idea of God's wrath. And that may be what bothers us the most. That God is a God who is angry with evil, at war with evil, livid with evil. It is as if we have determined

God has no right to any emotion but love. And, if he does express anger, we have a bad or immoral God on our hands. But why does an angry God bother us so much? I once read some penetrating words on this from Yale theologian Miroslav Volf. He was born in Croatia and lived through the nightmare years of ethnic strife in the former Yugoslavia—a time that included the destruction of churches, the raping of women, and the murdering of innocents. He once thought that wrath and anger were beneath God, but he said he came to realize that his view of God had been too low:

> I used to think that wrath was unworthy of God. Isn't God love? Shouldn't divine love be beyond wrath? God is love, and God loves every person and every creature. That's exactly why God is wrathful against some of them. My last resistance to the idea of God's wrath was a casualty of the war in the former Yugoslavia, the region from which I come. According to some estimates, 200,000 people were killed and over 3,000,000 were displaced. *My* villages and cities were destroyed, *my* people shelled day in and day out, some of them brutalized beyond imagination, and I could not imagine God not being angry. Or think of Rwanda in the last decade of the past century, where 800,000 people were hacked to death in one hundred days! How did God react to the carnage? By doting on the perpetrators in a grandfatherly fashion? By refusing to condemn the bloodbath but instead affirming the perpetrators' basic goodness? Wasn't God fiercely angry with them? Though I used to complain about the indecency of the idea of God's wrath, I came to think that I would have to rebel against a God who *wasn't* wrathful at the sight of the world's evil. God isn't wrathful in spite of being love. God is wrathful *because* God is love.[23]

Yes.

When it comes to God, the fire that warms can be the fire that burns. I'm not sure any other kind of God would even matter.

3

JESUS 101

"But what about you?" he asked. "Who do you say I am?"

Jesus (Matt. 16:15)

He was born in a small, obscure village of somewhat questionable repute, the child of a peasant woman. He didn't go to high school or college. In fact, he never traveled more than two hundred miles from the place where he was born. He never wrote a book. He never held public office. And he was only thirty-three years old when the tide of public opinion turned against him, prompting even his closest friends to abandon him. He was then turned over to his enemies and was nailed to a wooden cross between two criminals. While he was dying, his executioners gambled for his clothing, the only property he had on earth. After he died, he was laid in a borrowed grave through the pity of an acquaintance.

Yet today, he is arguably the central figure of the entire human race. His life even marks our concept of time. We call this AD 2019, Latin for *anno Domini*, "the year of our Lord." Anything before that is referenced by BC, meaning, "before Christ." As

Philip Yancey observed about the life of Jesus, "You can gauge the size of a ship that has passed out of sight by the huge wake it leaves behind."[1] No wonder that everyone, no matter where they are spiritually, is intrigued by Jesus and fascinated by his life and his teaching, message, and mission.

Historicity

Let's begin with the most obvious question to consider: Did Jesus even exist? Are we talking about someone who is real or is he a myth?[2] Actually, this one is easy to check off the list. No scholar, no matter where they stand on Christianity itself, denies that the man Jesus, the one the Bible talks about, existed in time and history. Jesus is one of the most documented figures in all of human history. You find him listed in the writings of Thallus, who was a first-century Greek writer; Pliny the Younger, a lawyer and author of ancient Rome; the Roman historians Tacitus and Suetonius; and the Jewish historian Flavius Josephus. Of course, the most detailed record is found in the Bible, which gives not one, but four independent, eyewitness biographical accounts written by the men Matthew, Mark, Luke, and John. More than a few historians have noted that his is the most documented life in all of ancient history.

So we know Jesus existed.

We also know a few other things for certain. We know that his teaching was of such a compelling nature that, to this day, it's part of our cultural ethos. Whether memorable lines such as "Do unto others as you would have them do unto you," or timeless stories like the prodigal son (which you can read in the New Testament of the Bible in Luke 15:11–32), no one has been more spiritually or culturally influential. We also know that miracles were attributed to him. Whether you buy into the possibility of miracles or not, people who witnessed his life said he did them. We know that after a public ministry he was sentenced to death through a Jewish and then Roman legal process. We know that on the third day after his execution there was an empty tomb. A stone was rolled away and the body was gone. Even the Romans owned that. Now, they had their version of what happened, which we'll explore soon, but that the tomb was empty is without a doubt. And we know his followers went running around the landscape saying that Jesus had risen from the dead and that they had seen him, talked with him, and touched him. This wasn't just one of the disciples making this claim, or even just a handful, but *all* of them. There are even records of groups numbering in the hundreds who witnessed the resurrected Jesus at the same time. After that first Easter, the Jesus movement exploded. By AD 100, there were around 25,000 followers. By AD 310, there were 20,000,000. And today, there are billions and Christianity is the world's largest religious faith.

So who was he . . . really?

What Did Jesus Look Like?

One of the things people seem to be the most curious about when it comes to Jesus is what he looked like. Is there a physical description of Jesus? The answer is, "Yes and no." First, the no. The Bible never says, "Jesus was white, 6'3", with blond hair and chiseled good looks." But here's the "yes" part. We do know that he *wasn't* white, 6'3", with blond hair and chiseled good looks. While there is not a single historical reference to the physical appearance of Jesus and nothing in the Bible that describes his looks, we do know that he was a Mediterranean Jew; therefore, his skin would have had the olive darkness to it that you find in that region to this day. This also means he didn't speak English. Not even King James English (sorry, he never uttered the words *thee* or *thou*). His native tongue was Aramaic. He would have been schooled as a boy in Hebrew and probably Greek, which was the common language of business and commerce, but when walking down the road with

BBC Photo Library

Forensic scientists used cultural and archaeological data to create what they think the face of Jesus looked like.

family, Aramaic was the language of choice. Being a Mediterranean Jew also means that he wasn't overly tall—probably well under six feet. And, according to the ancient prophecies surrounding the coming of the Messiah that Christians believe apply to Jesus, he wasn't physically impressive at all. In fact, the prophet Isaiah wrote in the Old Testament of the Bible that "he had no beauty or majesty to attract us to him, nothing in his appearance that we should desire him" (Isa. 53:2). So the idea that Jesus

Painting of *Christ Pantocrator* in the Church of the Pater Noster, Jerusalem

was "tall, dark, and handsome" is only accurate on the "dark" part.

The earliest drawing ever made of him, at least the earliest that is still in existence, dates to the fifth century. The original hangs in one of the most ancient Christian structures on Earth, St. Catherine's Monastery in the Sinai desert of Egypt. It's called the *Christ*

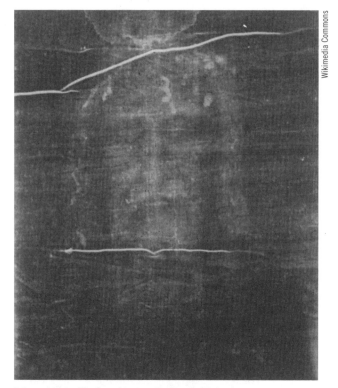

Enhanced photo of the face of Jesus on the Shroud of Turin

Pantocrator, translated "Christ Almighty." It is the classic picture of Christ that dominated ancient Christianity and continues to be displayed in many churches to this day.

While the picture is ancient, we are far from certain Jesus looked like this. Forensic anthropologists have tried to re-create what Jesus might have actually looked like from common skeletal remains of that era and region. The image they came up with is not particularly flattering, but would fit the biblical prophecies as well as the distinguishing features of his actual ethnicity.[3]

But if you want to go all the way back, the earliest possible image we have (hotly debated in terms of authenticity) is the famed Shroud of Turin. It is thought to be the shroud the body of Jesus was wrapped in following his crucifixion, and that miraculously carries his image to this day.

In truth, we don't know what he looked like beyond being short, dark skinned, and without any shot of being named *People* magazine's Sexiest Man Alive.

What Was His Childhood Like?

A second set of questions many have about Jesus relate to his childhood: What was it like? What was he like as a child? What was life like for him growing up? There's not a lot of information to be found here. Most of the biographical material we have begins with his birth and then leapfrogs to his thirtieth year, when he began his public ministry. But there are some things that we do know that might be of interest.

First, it is helpful to be reminded of what the heart of the Christian faith maintains: Jesus is God himself in human form, God the Son, the second person of the Trinity. One of the most amazing teachings in the Bible about God is the idea that God is triune. That his very nature is trinity. The Bible teaches the oneness of God—there are not many gods, but only One God. But then the Bible follows that up with another teaching: there are three persons who are each referred to as God—God the Father, God the Son, and God the Holy Spirit. Not three gods, but three persons who are one God. So you find Jesus referring to God the Father, but then referring to himself as God as well. And he was God the Son. To be the "son" of someone in the way Jesus was referring to meant to be of the same order as that person, and to have the same qualities as that person. This is mind-boggling to think about on so many levels, but just consider it in terms of God really becoming human, starting off with becoming a baby. Philip Yancey writes that the God who could have roared, "who could order armies and empires about like pawns on a chessboard, this

God emerged . . . as a baby who could not speak or eat solid food or control his bladder, [and] who depended on a [poor] teenage [mother] for shelter, food and love."[4]

This means the childhood of Jesus was very much like any other child's. Max Lucado writes that once born, he had to have his diaper changed. When he hit puberty, he had pimples. He may have been tone-deaf. Perhaps a girl down the street had a crush on him. It could have been that his knees were bony, or that he had a cowlick in his hair that Mary, his mother, could never do anything with. He was completely divine, but he was also completely human. But that raises all kinds of questions, doesn't it? This child who was God in human form—what was that like? Lucado made a list of questions he'd like to ask Mary:

What was it like watching him pray?

Did you ever feel awkward teaching him how he created the world?

Did he ever come home with a black eye?

Did he do well in school?

Did he ever have to ask a question about Scripture?

Who was his best friend?

Did you ever think, *That's God eating my soup?*[5]

So what do we know about those early years in Jesus's life? Well, we know he was raised in poverty. We know this from a scene that took place on the fortieth day after his birth. His parents, Mary and Joseph, took him to Jerusalem to present him at the Temple. You see, in Jesus's day, following the birth of a son, a mother had to wait forty days before going to the Temple to offer a sacrifice for the purpose of her purification. The intent was to consecrate the baby to God. Back then, it was usually just the firstborn who was dedicated in this way, for it was the firstborn who had all the rights of inheritance. As part of the dedication, it was common

The *Presentation of Jesus in the Temple* by Francesco Vittore Carpaccio at the Gallerie dell'Accademia in Venice, Italy

for the parents to give a sacrifice or an offering. In the Bible we are told that Mary and Joseph chose to offer a pair of doves (or a pair of pigeons), which indicates they were poor. The best and most common sacrifice was a lamb, and the only reason to offer a substitute was if you didn't have the money for a lamb. This required securing special approval for a pair of doves or a pigeon to be accepted—a recognition that you were so poor you couldn't afford anything else. Mary and Joseph apparently did this, so we know they were poor.

Another significant fact we know about his childhood is that he was raised in the town of Nazareth. It was not a large place, just a little village. And not a very good one. Nazareth didn't carry a good reputation. If I told you I came from Bangladesh, Nigeria, or Syria, images of poverty, violence, or unrest would probably instantly come to mind. Nazareth had a bad social reputation, as well. The people were seen as backward, illiterate, and poor. Later, in the Bible's record of the life of Jesus, you read that when people heard him referred to as Jesus of Nazareth (that's how people were identified then—their first name and where they were from), they said, "Nazareth! Can anything good come from there?" (John 1:46). Even the name *Nazarene* in that day was synonymous with someone who was despised. Let's just say he came from the wrong side of the tracks.

Another dynamic of Jesus's childhood that a lot of people either don't know or don't think about is how he was raised by a single-parent mother during his formative teenage years. He didn't have Joseph as his father for very long. One of the better-known details about Mary is that when she was betrothed to Joseph and received her angelic visit about giving birth to Jesus as a virgin, she was young. In that day, engagement usually took place immediately after entering puberty, so Mary would have just entered her teens—as in thirteen, fourteen, or, at the most, fifteen. But what isn't as well known is that while Mary was young, Joseph was old. So theirs was what is known as a May-December romance. And by our standards, very May and very December. He was probably in his thirties or forties and, as mentioned, she may have been as young as thirteen. But this would not have been uncommon for that day.[6]

Then, whether it was because of his age or illness or both, sometime after Jesus turned twelve Joseph apparently died. The last record of Joseph is when Jesus was twelve, when he and Mary took Jesus to the Temple. The next scene from the life of Jesus, found in all four biographical accounts of his life in the Bible, is when he was thirty and began his public ministry. And in all four accounts, not a word is mentioned of Joseph. When Jesus returns home, when Jesus interacts with Mary—no Joseph. He is never present at any event in Jesus's adult life, even when the rest of Jesus's family is there. And on the cross, before his death, Jesus asks a man named John, who was also one of his closest friends and followers, to watch over Mary. This intimates that Jesus, as the eldest son, had carried that responsibility to that point and now was asking another family member (John may have been a cousin of Jesus) to watch over his mother. This tells us that Mary was a widow, and that sometime between the ages of twelve and thirty, probably in Jesus's teen years, Joseph had died. Regardless of exactly when he died, or what filled his life before this marriage, his death explains why Jesus didn't begin his public ministry until the age of thirty. He was providing for the family, carrying on as a carpenter as taught by his father. He assumed the role of caregiver until his brothers were able to assume primary care for their mother and the other siblings.

Did He Have Brothers and Sisters?

This brings us to another common question: Did Jesus have brothers and sisters? As you read just a moment ago, yes, he had brothers. Christians believe his brothers were half-brothers through Mary, since he was conceived of the Holy Spirit through a virginal conception, part of the miracle surrounding Christ as the God-Man. Probably the most famous of Jesus's siblings was James, who wrote the part of the New Testament of the Bible known as the book of James. James was a later son of Mary and Joseph, and head of the Jerusalem church. He was one of the select individuals Jesus appeared to after his resurrection. He was called a "pillar" of the early church, meaning someone who was instrumental in building it, keeping it up, making it strong. Another famed follower of Jesus, a man by the name of Paul, was used by God to write much of the New Testament. On Paul's first visit to Jerusalem, he went immediately to see James, acknowledging the influential nature of his leadership in the early church. When the early church leader Peter was rescued from prison, Peter told his friends to be sure and tell James. Tradition has it that he was known as "old camel knees," because thick calluses built up on his knees from many years of determined prayer. Tradition also has it that he was martyred through a beheading around AD 62 under the great persecution of Christians by the Roman emperor Nero.

When Did He Know He Was God?

So if Jesus was a normal child who was fully human but also fully God, when did he discover the God side of things? Was he born with some kind of weird maturity so that he knew it from day one? Did it come to him sometime during puberty? Did it happen when he was baptized by the man known as John the Baptist at age thirty, when he began his public ministry? When did Jesus know that he could walk on the water he had to take a bath in?

Nobody knows.

But we have a hint that he knew by the time of puberty, the time of his coming of age, which would have been around twelve. We know this because of the only scene recorded in the Bible about his adolescent years. It's worth reading:

Every year Jesus' parents went to Jerusalem for the Passover festival. When Jesus was twelve years old, they attended the festival as usual. After the celebration was over, they started home to Nazareth, but Jesus stayed behind in Jerusalem. His parents didn't miss him at first, because they assumed he was among the other travelers. But when he didn't show up that evening, they started looking for him among their relatives and friends.

When they couldn't find him, they went back to Jerusalem to search for him there. Three days later they finally discovered him in the Temple, sitting among the religious teachers, listening to them and asking questions. All who heard him were amazed at his understanding and his answers.

His parents didn't know what to think. "Son," his mother said to him, "why have you done this to us? Your father and I have been frantic, searching for you everywhere."

"But why did you need to search?" he asked. "Didn't you know that I must be in my Father's house?" But they didn't understand what he meant.

Then he returned to Nazareth with them and was obedient to them. And his mother stored all these things in her heart.

Jesus grew in wisdom and in stature and in favor with God and all the people. (Luke 2:41–52 NLT)

At twelve, Jesus went to the Temple and stayed there day and night. He demonstrated a wisdom and intelligence, a spiritual maturity and insight that was unnatural. He was already amazing people at twelve. And though his parents were frantic, he knew they shouldn't have been. He knew they should have known where he would be—in his Father's house. And even that sentence is significant. The Jews of that day would never have simply said "my Father." That was too informal, too intimate. They would have said "our Father," or even more likely, "our Father in heaven." But not Jesus. Just "my Father." So it would seem that at this time, he knew who he was. It also appears that this knowledge was something he grew into, matured into, and gained an ever-increasing understanding of, as his physical, human life developed. Notice that last line again of the verses above, noting how Jesus matured, growing up in both wisdom and stature.

Was He Ever Married?

So when he grew up, was there a Mrs. Jesus? One of the most common myths surrounding the life of Jesus is that he got married and had children. That's not surprising since a bestselling novel in modern history, Dan Brown's *The Da Vinci Code*, made that idea its central premise.

At first glance, the plot wasn't anything that stood out above the normal mystery fare. The murder of a curator at the Louvre in Paris leads to a trail of clues found in the work of Leonardo da Vinci and to the discovery of a centuries-old secret society. But that's not what grabbed our collective cultural attention. Brown went on to write that the clues in Leonardo's work and the mission of the secret society revolved around the Holy Grail. This was not referring to the chalice Jesus used during the Last Supper. The novel suggested that the Holy Grail was instead a reference to the bloodline of Jesus. That a woman named Mary Magdalene was the wife of Jesus and the mother of his child. And because she bore descendants, specifically a daughter named Sarah, she was, in fact, the Holy Grail. In the novel, Mary fled after the crucifixion with Sarah to the south of France, where they established the Merovingian line of European royalty. This became the basis for the secret society to preserve the bloodline and protect the secret until it was time to make it known to the world.

The problem with all of this is that Brown contended that he was basing his entire book on fact. So was he? Not according to every reputable scholar on the planet. First, about Mary Magdalene. The Bible states that Mary was a devoted follower of Christ, liberated from a serious illness of some kind that had plagued her life. She was present at his crucifixion and burial and was the first person Jesus appeared to following his resurrection. She was even charged to bring the news of his resurrection to his disciples, which she did. She was a remarkable woman, prominently featured in the New Testament of the Bible and honored throughout Christian history. But married to Jesus or a secret lover? There is absolutely no evidence that indicates Mary had a relationship with Jesus beyond being a devoted spiritual follower. Karen King, a history professor at Harvard University, while never claiming that Jesus was married put forward the possibility of evidence that, after the time of Jesus, people believed he might have been. She now admits there is no evidence for that.[7]

What Did Jesus Say about Himself?

This brings us to the most significant thing to know about Jesus, and it has to do with what Jesus said about himself. It was very direct:

> The Jews [said to Jesus], "Aren't we right in saying that you are a Samaritan and demon-possessed?"
>
> "I am not possessed by a demon," said Jesus. . . . "Very truly I tell you, whoever obeys my word will never see death."
>
> At this they exclaimed, "Now we know that you are demon-possessed! Abraham died and so did the prophets, yet you say that whoever obeys your word will never taste death. Are you greater than our father Abraham? He died, and so did the prophets. Who do you think you are?"
>
> Jesus replied, ". . . Your father Abraham rejoiced at the thought of seeing my day; he saw it and was glad."
>
> "You are not yet fifty years old," they said to him, "and you have seen Abraham!"

"Very truly I tell you," Jesus answered, "before Abraham was born, I am!" At this, they picked up stones to stone him. (John 8:48–49, 51–54, 56–59)

Who did Jesus say he was? He referred to himself here as "I am." Now that's either very bad grammar or he was trying to say something very significant.

Let's explore the significance.

The background of "I am" is found in one of the most famous stories in the Bible, the story of Moses before the burning bush. The entire story of Moses is amazing, which is why almost every movie made on the Bible is either on Moses or Jesus. As a Hebrew baby, he was put in a small boat-like crib on the Nile to avoid being killed, rescued by the daughter of the pharaoh of Egypt, raised as a prince, sent into exile after killing a man who was assaulting a fellow Hebrew—and we haven't even come to the plagues, the parting of the sea, or the Ten Commandments. But back to "I am."

God himself was speaking to Moses, telling him to go to the highest authority and power in the land and demand that he release all of his Hebrew slaves. Moses understandably wanted to have a little credibility, so he asked God to give him his name—the very name of God—so that he could say to the people exactly who had sent him. Here's the answer God gave to Moses: "God said to Moses, 'I AM WHO I AM. This is what you are to say . . . : "I AM has sent me to you"'" (Exod. 3:14). That phrase—"I AM"—is considered the most holy word in existence because it is the very name of God. It was considered so holy that the Jews would not even write it completely, penning only the four consonants: "YHWH." Scholars used to think it was pronounced "Je-ho-vah." We now know that the closest we can make of the actual name in light of the missing vowels is that it was pronounced "Yah-weh."

God said my name is "Yahweh"—"I AM."

Now, return to what Jesus said when asked about his identity: "'Very truly I tell you,' Jesus answered, 'before Abraham was born,

I am!'" (John 8:58). Jesus claimed the very name of God for himself. He said, "You want to know who I am? I'll tell you—I am God." And the people listening understood him completely. They picked up stones to stone him, because this was nothing less than blasphemy. Here a mere man was claiming to be God himself. But this "mere man" made that claim repeatedly throughout his life. Here's a taste from some of the biographical records:

> I am the Son of God. (John 10:36 TLB)

> I am the way, the truth, and the life. (John 14:6 GNT)

> The high priest asked him, "Are you the Messiah, the Son of the Blessed One?"
> "I am," said Jesus. (Mark 14:61–62)

> Anyone who has seen me has seen the Father. (John 14:9)

So in Jesus, we have a person who walked the earth and claimed to be God. No other major religious figure has ever made that claim—not Buddha, not Mohammed, not Confucius. Only Jesus made the claim to be God in human form. So what do you do with that? As has often been observed, there are only four options.

First, you can conclude that Jesus was a stark raving lunatic. Maybe he *did* think he was God, but he was severely sick psychologically. The problem is that in most cases of severe psychological disorder, the background of the person makes it very clear they had a profile and history of mental illness. But nothing in the historical record of the life of Jesus exhibits a single sign of any of the classical manifestations of mental illness, such as the inability to relate to the real world, inadequacy in personal relationships, or deficiencies in verbal skills. In fact, psychiatrist J. T. Fisher concluded that if you were to survey all of the psychological data that Jesus's life has to offer, and boil it down to one essential and perfect prescription for mental health, it would be the Sermon on the Mount—the most famous single message Jesus ever proclaimed.[8]

A second choice is to say he was simply a liar. Jesus said he was God but obviously knew he wasn't. But this would be saying that the man whose teaching has set the standard for integrity and honesty throughout the civilized world was a habitual, premeditated, pathological liar. Even more important to remember is that Jesus was arrested, mocked, beaten, and tortured prior to his execution. Willingly. Jesus was offered a full pardon by the Roman governor, Pilate, if he would simply deny his claim to be God. If a con man could stop a nail being driven into the flesh of his hand by telling the truth, you would think he would. People who are playing the system for personal gain tend to change their game when it stops paying off. They keep up the lie until the deception costs them more than what they gained through the deceit. But Jesus endured it all. He never denied his claim to be God, though given every chance.

A third option is to say that Jesus was just a good man, maybe even a prophet from God, but that's all. Not many people want to say that Jesus was a lunatic or a liar, but they don't want to say he was God in human flesh, either. So they land on him being simply a good man, a holy man—no more. But there's a problem with this option as well. Here's what C. S. Lewis wrote about this idea:

> I am trying here to prevent anyone saying the really foolish thing that people often say about Him: "I'm ready to accept Jesus as a great moral teacher, but I don't accept His claim to be God." That is the one thing we must not say. A man who was merely a man and said the sort of things Jesus said would not be a great moral teacher. He would either be a lunatic—on a level with the man who says he is a poached egg—or else he would be the Devil of Hell. You must make your choice. Either this man was, and is, the Son of God: or else a madman or something worse. You can shut him up for a fool, you can spit at Him and kill Him as a demon; or you can fall at His feet and call Him Lord and God. But let us not come with

any patronising nonsense about His being a great human teacher. He has not left that open to us. He did not intend to.[9]

Lewis is right. Here we have a man who walked the earth and claimed to be God in human form. You can say that Jesus was insane—that the man who has, in the minds of many, given the world its greatest picture of sanity was in fact a stark raving lunatic. You can say that Jesus was a liar—that the man whose teaching has set the standard for integrity and honesty in the civilized world was a habitual, premeditated, pathological deviant.

Or you can fall at his feet and call him Lord, which is, of course, the last of our four options. What you can't say is that Jesus was just a good man, maybe even a prophet, but that's all. That is one option he didn't give.

Why Did He Pray to God If He Was God?

So if you're adding all this up, you may have a nagging question about Jesus's identity: Why did he pray to God if he was God? And make no mistake, he did. A lot. So who was he praying to? Remember our earlier conversation about the nature of God being triune? The Trinity means that God *is* community, the perfect relationship between the Father and the Son and the Holy Spirit. Here's how Brent Curtis and John Eldredge describe it:

> Think of your best moments of love or friendship or creative partnership, the best times with family or friends around the dinner table, your richest conversations, the acts of simple kindness that sometimes seem like the only things that make life worth living. Like the shimmer of sunlight on a lake, these are reflections of the love that flows among the Trinity. We long for intimacy because we are made in the image of perfect intimacy.[10]

Or as the thirteenth-century theologian and philosopher Meister Eckhart wrote, "We were created out of the laughter of the

Trinity."[11] So that's why you have Jesus—God the Son—praying, talking, and communicating with God the Father.

So Why Did He Come?

So why did God come to Earth in the person of Jesus? Danish philosopher Søren Kierkegaard writes of the risk and complexity of this divine desire through the tale of a king:

> Suppose there was a king who loved a humble maiden. . . . Every statesman feared his wrath and dared not breathe a word of displeasure; every foreign state trembled before his power and dared not omit sending ambassadors with congratulations for the nuptials. . . . Then there awoke in the heart of the king an anxious thought. . . . Would she be happy in the life at his side? Would she be able to summon confidence enough never to remember . . . that he was a king and she had been a humble maiden? For if this memory were to waken in her soul, and like a favored lover sometimes steal her thoughts away from the king, luring her reflections into the seclusion of a silent grief . . . where would then be the glory of their love?[12]

The king wanted true love, but how could her love for him be true? He could bring her to the palace, covering her body with silk and jewels in an effort to coax affection by blinding her eyes.

But this would be a purchased heart.

He could come to her cottage, casting a pall of glory and power over its humble surroundings, driving her to her knees in awe and wonder.

But that would be an overpowered heart.

No, neither elevation of her nor himself could achieve the desired end. Only his own descent. Thus the king becomes a humble servant and seeks to win her heart, for only if it is so won has it been truly given at all.

God could have *made* us love him, but if he had, his relationship with us—and ours with him—would have been meaningless. As

I've said before, God wants our relationship with him and with others to be real. So he came to us.

As Jesus.

The Great Test

But how can we *know* if this story is true? If I told you that I was God in human form, come to earth to show the way and call the world back to myself, you would have every right to say, "Prove it." People certainly said that to Jesus and, rumor has it, he did prove it through a stunning array of miracles. From walking on water to raising the dead, Jesus silenced more than his fair share of skeptics. But he raised the stakes even further. He laid out a very specific "proof" for his claims that he invited anyone and everyone to judge him by. Christians believe he passed that ultimate litmus test and the entire world is still talking about it. His big proof? Coming back to life after death. He told people all along it was what he was going to do, and that it was going to be the definitive validation that he was who he said he was.

Let me give you a taste of his words:

> One day some teachers of religious law and Pharisees came to Jesus and said, "Teacher, we want you to show us a miraculous sign to prove your authority."
> But Jesus replied, ". . . The only sign I will give . . . is the sign of the prophet Jonah. For as Jonah was in the belly of the great fish for three days and three nights, so will the Son of Man be in the heart of the earth for three days and three nights." (Matt. 12:38–40 NLT)

> Some Pharisees and Sadducees were on him again, pressing him to prove himself to them. He told them, "You have a saying that goes, 'Red sky at night, sailor's delight; red sky at morning, sailors take warning.' You find it easy enough to forecast the weather—why can't you read the signs of the times? . . . The only sign you'll get is the Jonah sign." (Matt. 16:1–4 Message)

The Church of the Holy Sepulcher in Jerusalem, said to be the spot of the empty tomb

Taking the twelve disciples aside, Jesus said, "Listen, we're going up to Jerusalem, where all the predictions of the prophets concerning the Son of Man will come true. He will be handed over to the Romans, and he will be mocked, treated shamefully, and spit upon. They will flog him with a whip and kill him, but on the third day he will rise again." (Luke 18:31–33 NLT)

Over and over again, Jesus made it clear that the one sign you could test him by was whether he would come back from the dead on the third day after his death. And because of that, whether he succeeded means everything. Even the Bible says it's everything. One of the leaders of the early church, Paul, wrote:

If there's no resurrection for Christ, everything we've told you is smoke and mirrors, and everything you've staked your life on is smoke and mirrors. Not only that, but we would be guilty of telling a string of barefaced lies about God, all these affidavits we passed on to you verifying that God raised up Christ—sheer fabrications, if there's no resurrection. . . . But the truth is that Christ *has* been raised up. (1 Cor. 15:13–15, 20 Message)

But is it the truth? Did he rise from the dead? J. Warner Wallace is a decorated homicide investigator. After completing training through the Los Angeles Sheriff's Department, Wallace joined the force in Torrance, working on the SWAT team on the gang detail and investigating robbery and homicide cases. Later, he became a founding member of the department's cold-case homicide unit assigned to crack murders nobody else had been able to solve. His natural street-honed skepticism served him well. He once said, "As a cop, if you believe everything people tell you, then you'd never arrest anyone." So for him, facts need to be solid, witnesses have to be credible, evidence must be persuasive, corroboration is always crucial, and alibis have to be dismantled.

And he's good—very good—at what he does. Wallace has been awarded the Police and Fire Medal of Valor "Sustained Superiority" award and the CopsWest award for his ability to get to the truth and solve crimes. He's so good that he's been featured on Court TV, NBC's *Dateline*, and other news outlets when they need expertise on what it takes to arrest killers who thought they got away with murder.

Then he decided to take on the coldest case of his life. One that didn't go back a few years, or even decades, but one that went back two millennia.

He took on the death and the resurrection of Jesus.

He was an atheist, didn't believe a resurrection had occurred, and wanted to figure out what did happen since his wife had started to dabble a little bit in Christianity. He spent six months of painstaking analysis employing everything he had mastered as a detective: resisting the influence of dangerous presuppositions, emphasizing the importance of abductive reasoning, respecting the nature of circumstantial evidence and the role it plays and does not play, evaluating the reliability of witnesses, examining the choice and meaning of language through forensic statement analysis, determining what's important evidentially, recognizing the rarity of true conspiracies, establishing reliability by tracing the evidence, getting comfortable with conclusions and, finally, distinguishing between possible alternatives and reasonable alternatives. At the end of his investigation, this cold-case specialist reached his conclusions: Christianity is true beyond a reasonable doubt; the resurrection actually happened. Today, Detective J. Warner Wallace is a committed Christian.[13]

So what was it he found?

There are certain facts any investigation of this nature has in its possession to begin with. We know that Jesus existed. We know that after a public ministry he was sentenced to death through Roman crucifixion. We know that on the third day, there was an empty tomb—the stone was rolled away and the body was gone. We also know that on the third day after his crucifixion, his followers were quite bold in saying that he had risen from the dead and that they had, in fact, seen him. From that starting point, let's put our detective hats on and look at all of our options.

Did the Disciples Steal the Body?

The first option is that the disciples—or followers of Jesus—stole the body and then spread the idea that he rose from the dead. Jesus had said he would rise from the dead on the third day; so, on the third day, they stole the body so that it would look like it really happened. That way they wouldn't look stupid for following him. If it became known that Jesus was a fake—that he didn't rise from the dead like he said he would—they would be the laughingstock of the entire Middle East. So they stole the body, hid it, and then *said* he rose from the dead. Assuming this option, there were never any post-resurrection appearances and no empty tomb. The body was probably devoured by dogs, following the fate of most crucified Roman criminals without the benefit of a burial cave.

This was actually the primary idea that the enemies of Jesus raised when news of the empty tomb first hit. After the first few tweets came out about Jesus rising from the dead, the news started to trend on Facebook, and the first Instagram of the empty tomb went viral, his enemies sent out a few social media messages of their own. Even the Bible takes note of this and records how the rumor got started. The biography written by Matthew in the New Testament says:

> A few of [the guards] went into the city and told the high priests everything that had happened. They called a meeting of the religious leaders and came up with a plan: They took a large sum of money and gave it to the soldiers, bribing them to say, "His disciples came in the night and stole the body while we were sleeping." They assured them, "If the governor hears about your sleeping on duty, we will make sure you don't get blamed." The soldiers took the bribe and did as they were told. That story, cooked up in the Jewish High Council, is still going around. (Matt. 28:11–15 Message)

The problem that story ran into *then* is the same one it runs into *now*. The tomb was protected by a full guard of Roman soldiers. A Roman guard contained up to sixteen highly trained, heavily armed, professional fighting men. You couldn't have just snuck by them during the night, because that would have required all sixteen guards to be asleep at the same time, including the ones posted to keep watch at the time of the supposed abduction. The Roman penalty for sleeping on guard duty was execution. Staying awake on duty was one of the highest values the Roman army held. So this would call for the most sacred vow and highest value of the Roman military to be uniformly discarded. But, even more important, rolling away a two-ton stone makes *noise*. Lots of noise. The kind of noise that wakes up sleeping Roman guards. All sixteen of them.

That's not even the biggest reason why this would be hard to believe. Let's say they pulled it off. Let's say they did sneak past the guards and somehow rolled the stone away without waking anyone, and then stole the body out from under the noses of the guards. A conspiracy theory of this nature must account for the fact that, according to all four independent biographical accounts recorded in the Bible, the first witnesses to the resurrection were women. This would never have been invented by even the *least* sophisticated conspirators who wanted to authenticate a failed religious leader, for Jewish courts did not even *accept* the testimony of female witnesses.

But there's something even more telling: How does this account for the amazing, overnight transformation of the disciples from a band of frightened, betrayal-oriented cowards into a group of radical revolutionaries who willingly risked their lives to spread the message of the risen Jesus? Would this have happened for what they knew to be a lie? Eleven of the twelve disciples who hypothetically stole the body died martyr deaths.[14] Meaning they willingly, purposefully died for their story. They laid down their lives claiming to be eyewitnesses to the risen Jesus. I say eleven of the twelve because of John. The Roman authorities tried to kill John but were unsuccessful, so he ended up being exiled to the island of Patmos. Regardless, each of the disciples was faced with a decisive moment: deny what you say about Jesus and his resurrection and live, or cling to your pathetic story and die the cruelest, most painful and vicious death possible. Every single disciple faced this test of torture and martyrdom for the sake of the truth of the resurrection of Christ and themselves as personal eyewitnesses, but they stood their ground. And it cost them everything.

Tradition tells us that John's brother James was beheaded; Matthew was slain with a combination battle-axe and spear; Philip was whipped, thrown into prison, and then crucified; Simon the Zealot was crucified; Peter was crucified in Rome; James (son of Alphaeus) was thrown from the pinnacle of the Temple in Jerusalem and then beaten to death with a fuller's club; Bartholomew was beaten and then crucified; Andrew was bound to a cross from where he preached to his persecutors until his death; Thomas was run through the body with a lance; Jude was shot with arrows and then crucified; and Matthias, who replaced Judas Iscariot (the disciple who betrayed Jesus), was stoned and then beheaded.[15] Now think about that for a minute. People will die for what they *believe* to be true—what they *think* is true—even though it may be false. We see that all the time. But people don't have a tendency to die for what they *know* is a lie. Yet each of these eyewitnesses to the resurrected Jesus went to their death saying: "Jesus has risen, and I saw him. Kill me if you must, but it happened." So did the disciples steal the body? The evidence makes that very hard to believe.

Did the Jewish or Roman Authorities Steal the Body?

A second option is to say that the Jewish or Roman authorities stole the body. The dilemma with this view is one that crime detectives ask all the time: What would the motive be? They were the ones who put guards at the tomb to make sure the body *wasn't* stolen. Their biggest *fear* was somebody stealing the body. That's public record, and even recorded in the Bible:

> The high priests and Pharisees arranged a meeting with Pilate. They said, "Sir, we just remembered that that liar announced while he was still alive, 'After three days I will be raised.' We've got to get that tomb sealed until the third day. There's a good chance his disciples will come and steal the corpse and then go around saying, 'He's risen from the dead.' Then we'll be worse off than before, the final deceit surpassing the first."
>
> Pilate told them, "You will have a guard. Go ahead and secure it the best you can." So they went out and secured the tomb, sealing the stone and posting guards." (Matt. 27:62–66 Message)

So do you see the motive problem? They understood Christianity to be an incredible threat against both Jewish authority and Roman rule. They had a vested interest in making sure people *didn't* believe that Jesus rose from the dead. The whole purpose of the crucifixion was to silence Jesus and demoralize his followers. The last thing they would do is steal the body to make it look like he rose from the dead, which would make him and the Christian movement more believable than ever. They wished they *did* have the body! They would have paraded it through the streets of Jerusalem, saying, "See, he was just a man. Here's his beat-up, crucified corpse." But they didn't. So did the Jewish or Roman authorities steal the body? That flies in the face of everything we know. This is also why nobody has ever seriously entertained the idea that the resurrection can be written off as some kind of mass hallucination due to people's grief or emotional stress, or that perhaps they mistook someone else (who was alive) for (the very dead) Jesus. Not only would a hallucination or mistaken sighting have to account for *every* single eyewitness account, but the simple production of a dead body by the Romans would have brought everyone back to reality.

The painting *Christ Crucified* by Diego Velazquez

Did They Just Go to the Wrong Tomb?

A third option is that the disciples just went to the wrong tomb. This option doesn't attract much attention from people who look carefully at the evidence but needs to be raised in order to be thorough. The thinking is that the disciples were nervous, worried, and full of fear. It would have been relatively easy for them to have simply made a mistake by going to the wrong tomb, finding that tomb empty, and then assuming that Jesus was alive. The problem with this view is that all the Romans would have had to do was point out the right tomb where the guards were posted and the party would have ended. And you still have to deal with all the people who said they saw Jesus after his death—people who were more than willing to go on record, even under threat of death. Consider these words written by the apostle Paul in his letter to the church in Corinth. He noted that Jesus "appeared to Cephas, and then to the Twelve. After that, he appeared to more than five hundred of the brothers and sisters at the same time, most of whom are still living. . . . Then he appeared to James, then to all the apostles, and last of all he appeared to me also" (1 Cor. 15:5–8). In today's court system, all it takes is one or two eyewitnesses to begin to determine what happened at a particular point and place in time. There were *hundreds* of eyewitnesses to Jesus being alive after his crucifixion. And again, all of the disciples said they saw him and were willing to die for it.

In fact, they did.

Did Jesus Really Die?

A fourth option is what has been called the "swoon theory." This was first suggested back in the late 1700s, and then gained attention in the 1960s through a book called *The Passover Plot*. This idea is a little different than the others; it says that Jesus never really died on the cross. He never resurrected, because he never died. This theory says that he was *mistakenly* reported to be dead when in reality, he just "swooned" or passed out on the cross from exhaustion, pain, and loss of blood. Or in the immortal words of Miracle Max from one of my favorite movies, *The Princess Bride*, he was just "mostly dead." And, as we all know, mostly dead means slightly alive. And from that slightly alive state, after three days he got up, walked around, claimed he rose from the dead, and was received as resurrected.

Even the most die-hard skeptics don't raise this option very often. First, it makes Jesus out to be the most manipulative, false, lying, deceitful religious figure in all of human history. Not many people feel that way about Jesus. But the big argument against the swoon theory is physical—meaning, what he had to survive.

One of the first things he endured was a savage flogging from the Roman guards. He received thirty-nine lashes with a form of cat-o'-nine-tails, with weighted pellets of lead at the end of the whip and ends that were embedded with bone and metal to add weight—along with razor-sharp hooks. It was designed so that when it hit your back, it dug in. When it was pulled back, whatever flesh was on the hook was ripped out, literally tearing the body apart, often leaving the bones and intestines showing. He received thirty-nine of these lashes. Forty, by Roman law, was considered the death penalty.

Then, he was pierced in the head with multiple wooden stakes. You may have heard that Jesus had a "crown of thorns" placed on his head or have seen pictures of this (like the previous image). But what was used then were date palms, and the thorns were several inches in length. So it wasn't placed on his head as much as his head was impaled on it. It would be like having a series of three- or four-inch nails driven into your skull, causing massive facial distortion. It was beaten into his skull with the equivalent of a baseball bat to drive the wood as deep into his head as possible. Without a doubt, that alone could have killed anyone.

He then was made to drag his heavy wooden cross all the way up to a hill called Golgotha, which is where he was to be crucified, until he collapsed and could carry it no farther. That indicates that by this time he was already so physically decimated that he couldn't even walk. He then was nailed to the wooden arms of the cross with spikes that would have been driven into his wrists. Medieval art shows the holes in his palms, but when the Bible says the nails went through his hands, the word used for "hands" translates as anywhere from the wrist up. Based on corpses found who were crucified during that time period, the nail was typically driven through the wrist so as not to tear through the flesh of the hand with the weight of the body hanging on the cross. The goal was for the body to hang. Nails were also driven through the ankle, among the most sensitive nerves that could have been pierced. This is where we get our word *excruciating*: literally "from the cross," a pain that is so severe it can only come from crucifixion. After suffering all of that, Jesus then hung on the cross until he essentially suffocated to death. You had to push yourself up against the spike in your ankles to breathe. Eventually the body tires of this and the person chokes to death. And finally, Jesus was pierced in the side with a lance to ensure death, and subsequently pronounced dead by Roman experts.

"Swoon" theorists would have us believe this happened next: after Jesus was laid in a damp tomb in burial clothes and seventy-five pounds of burial spices, and endured three days without food, water, or medical attention of any kind, he popped up and said, "I feel better!" He rolled back a stone weighing thousands of pounds, then single-handedly, without any kind of weapon, overpowered a crack team of Rome's heavily armed, heavily armored, elite fighting troops. He then started walking around town, looking, physically, like pretty much nothing happened—just a few holes here and there but otherwise none the worse for wear.

The resurrection is easier to believe than that.

But even more telling is that medical experts have pored over the biblical record of Jesus's death. There was even an article in the *Journal of the American Medical Association* titled, "On the Physical Death of Jesus Christ." Among the article's points is that the Bible records, with great detail, that when the spear pierced Jesus's side, water *and* blood spilled out. Though the eyewitnesses who recorded that didn't know it at the time, we now know this was a medically significant detail. It was a sign that the spear pierced the pericardium, which is the sac that surrounds the heart, as well as the heart itself. It is a description of the postmortem separation of the blood into clot and serum, indicating that Jesus was truly dead.[16]

So Are You Saying He Rose from the Dead?

So let's add this up. If the disciples didn't steal the body, the Jewish and Roman authorities didn't steal the body, there wasn't any kind of mass hallucination, they didn't go to the wrong tomb, and Jesus didn't just pass out on the cross and start feeling better in a day or two . . . what option is left? Christians have concluded that he did what he said he was going to do. Why? Because he was who he said he was.

He rose from the dead.

Now, I know that you might be thinking: *Time out! I don't care what the evidence points to. You're not going to back me into this corner through some kind of hypothetical detective analysis. Dead people don't rise!*

And you're right. They don't. We know that now and they knew it then. But that's the point.

This is what startled N. T. Wright, who taught at both Cambridge and Oxford. In his massive, 800-plus-page academic work on the history surrounding the resurrection event of Jesus, he writes that no one would have ever thought up the resurrection, because nobody believed such a thing possible. Nowhere in paganism, nowhere in Judaism, nowhere in any worldview or philosophy did anybody ever conceive, posit, contemplate, or even suggest that such a thing could—or ever had—taken place. Wright's conclusion is that "the early Christians did not invent the empty tomb and the 'meetings' or 'sightings' of the risen Jesus in order to explain a faith they already had. They developed that faith."[17] And why did they develop it? Because of what they saw, because of what they experienced, because what they didn't think was going to happen—or could happen—*did* happen.

So What?

This isn't an intellectual game. If it happened, it validates Jesus and everything he taught. But there's more. If it happened to him, it also means it can happen to us. To *you*. If true, two thousand years ago the power of God was reflected in a single life with such a clear demonstration of might and energy that all of human history was forever changed—culminating in raising that life, physically, from the dead. And through the resurrection of Jesus, God demonstrated his ultimate power, because there is no greater power on earth than power over death. Then the Bible says something equally radical: the very same power that raised Jesus from the dead is available for *your* life. Here are its words and the promise that goes with them: "[You need to] understand the incredible greatness of God's power for us who believe him. This is the same mighty power that raised Christ from the dead" (Eph. 1:19–20 NLT). The word for power used in that verse in the original Greek language was the word *dunamis*, which is where we get our word *dynamite*. It's the same word used when referring to the power behind Jesus's miracles. And, as we just read, the power that raised him from the dead.

That's some power.

And the Bible says that power can be there for you. Think about that. That means the power that resurrected Jesus can resurrect your life too. Not just after you die a physical death, but here and now! God can take your life, and no matter where you are or where you've been, he can bring you to life from any place you feel lifeless. He can give you whatever new beginning you need. Here's how the Bible puts it: "And just as Christ was raised from the dead by the glorious power of the Father, now we also may live new lives" (Rom. 6:4 NLT).

Beyond a new life, Christians believe that the resurrection of Jesus can give us the power we need to live the way God wants us to live. We live in a day of self-help websites and seminars, apps and tech toys. Such resources and experiences are good for telling us what we are supposed to do, but they can't give us the power to do it. The Bible promises an external power source, claiming that the power to change our life can come to us from God. We don't have it within us to live the way we want to live, much less the way we are supposed to live. But the Bible says that the very same power that raised Jesus from the dead is available for your life. You may not be ready to have it, or even believe it, but millions of Christians can testify to the fact that God's power has altered their lives. Marriages that seemed beyond hope have been restored. Long, habitual, destructive patterns of behavior have been broken. Finances have been straightened out, difficulties on the job have been overcome, and parenting challenges have been met. The resurrection of Jesus matters because it reveals to us that the power of God is there to change our life.

Even that's not the best of the "so what" when it comes to the resurrection of Jesus. In a letter to a group of Christians who had just chosen to put their trust in Jesus, the early Christian leader Paul reminded them of one more dynamic of the resurrection: "If all we get out of Christ is a little inspiration for a few short years, we're a pretty sorry lot. But the truth is that Christ *has* been raised up, the first in a long legacy of those who are going to leave the cemeteries" (1 Cor. 15:19–20 Message).

The Bible says that if there was no resurrection, then there's no hope for life after death. And if that's true, then life has no purpose and no meaning. Søren Kierkegaard once compared such a view to a smooth, flat stone that is thrown over the surface of a pond. The stone dances and skims over the surface of the water until that moment comes when, like life without hope beyond death, it runs out of momentum and sinks into nothingness.[18] In a similar vein, Samuel Beckett once put forth a play titled *Breath*. The curtain opens to a stage littered with nothing but garbage. A soundtrack begins, starting with a baby's first cry and ending with an old man's last, dying gasp. Then the curtain closes. Beckett's point is clear—life is absurd, man is meaningless, existence is pointless. But Christianity maintains that the resurrection *did* happen, and the Bible says that "because Jesus was raised from the dead, we've been given a brand-new life and have everything to live for, including a future in heaven" (1 Pet. 1:3 Message).

And that means hope. But that hope involves embracing a message—a message unlike any ever given.

4

THE MESSAGE

Even those who have renounced Christianity and attack it, in their inmost being still follow the Christian ideal, for hitherto neither their subtlety nor the ardour of their hearts has been able to create a higher ideal of man and of virtue than the ideal given by Christ.

Dostoevsky, *The Brothers Karamazov*

There was a British conference on comparative religions that brought together experts from all over the world to debate what was unique, if anything, about the Christian faith in relation to other religions. Was it the idea that a god became a man? No, other religions had variations on that one. Even the Greek myths were about gods appearing in human form. Was it heaven, life after death, or an eternal soul? Was it love for your neighbor, good works, care for the poor or homeless? Was it about sin or hell or judgment? The debate went on for some time, until C. S. Lewis wandered into the room. (As we read earlier, Lewis journeyed from atheism to agnosticism and then eventually to Christianity and became one of the most famous of all Christian writers and thinkers from his positions at Oxford and Cambridge.) Lewis asked what the debate was about and found out that his colleagues were discussing what Christianity's unique contribution was among world religions.

"Oh, that's easy," he said. "It's grace."

And after they thought about it, they had to agree. The heart of the Christian message is the heart of the message Jesus brought to the world: grace, coupled with truth. We tend to get truth. But what is grace? We use the word in so many ways, seldom in the way Jesus used it. And the only way to understand his use of the word is to understand why we need this message so desperately. So let's get at the "why" before the "what." In other words, let's start with why grace is such a unique and needed message. To do that, you have to understand five background issues: the nature of God, the law of God, the human condition, the Old Testament sacrificial system, and then Jesus himself. If this sounds daunting or, even worse, dry, I promise I'll move fast. But trust me, each is important. Consider the five of them, together, Christian Theology 101.

First, the nature of God. What you need to understand about the nature of God is his holiness and his love. God is truly perfect and holy—sin is repulsive to him. He is allergic to it and cannot look upon it. His holiness demands either the removal or destruction of sin. But God is also love. Which means that much of the activity and any understanding of God lies at the crossroads of holiness and love. It's the creative tension of all that he is and does.

The second thing to understand is the law—God's spiritual and moral law. I know, *law* is not a positive word for many of us. Think of it here not as an arbitrarily set policy but rather as a manifestation of what *is* right or wrong: God's standards and his dictates—the very expression of God's person and God's will. The law *is* God and God *is* the law. It is his very nature and his character. As a result, it is God we either obey or disobey. When we obey it is an act of love, and when we disobey it is an attack on God's very nature. Cosmic treason. And the penalty is serious—

the most serious of all—which is why in the New Testament book of Romans, the Bible offers these words: "for the wages of sin is death" (Rom. 6:23). We are familiar with the reality of physical death, but the Bible also teaches the reality of spiritual death, which is separation from God. Sin causes spiritual death. It breaks the relationship. It destroys the intimacy that God intended to take place between himself and his creation because at its heart, sin is rebellion against God and his character. So punishment or consequences are not simply a possibility, but an inevitability.

This brings us to the issue of the human condition—all of us are sinners. We all have this sin condition and we cannot save ourselves or lift ourselves out of our sinfulness. The word *sin* is an archery term, and it literally means to "miss the mark." In archery, if you shoot an arrow toward a target and miss, it is called a sin. It doesn't matter whether it is by an inch or by a mile, it is still a sin. With that image in mind, take notice of how the Bible describes the human condition: "For everyone has sinned; we all fall short of God's glorious standard" (Rom. 3:23 NLT). When it comes to living life the way God intended, all of us "miss the mark." Some of us do better than others, but no one hits the bull's-eye every time. And sin isn't just about a failure to be perfect. Sin is about willful choices and conscious decisions that we make to knowingly go against God's leadership. It is the choice we make with our very soul to go against the moral law and will of God. So whether it's murder or malice, lust or lying, stealing or slander, it's falling short. And we can't change that. We can't address this. We can't fix it. We are totally unable to rescue ourselves from our sinful condition. Salvation by works is impossible. There's nothing *we* can do to right ourselves before God.

The fourth background issue to understand is the Old Testament sacrificial system. In ancient times, God decreed that the payment for wrongdoing—for a sin—could be covered through the blood of an animal. Though our rebellion deserved death, God's love allowed for our sin to be addressed through the sacrifice of an animal. That seems strange to us, but it was very intentional by God. He wanted people to see the severity of their sin. He wanted people to see that paying for the sin that comes between them and him is messy, gruesome, and costly, because sin is messy and gruesome and costly. And that it really was a life-or-death issue, so the symbol was a real one. The sacrifice was a substitute for the sinner; it bore the sinner's guilt and is where we get our term *scapegoat*. I'm sure you've heard of making someone the scapegoat for something—blaming them or pinning something on them. The term comes from the Bible. There was an annual Day of Atonement when a priest made reparations for all the sins of the people. The scapegoat was the goat to which the sins of the Israelites were symbolically transferred on that Day of Atonement. For the sacrifice to be effective, there had to be some kind of connection, some point of commonality between the victim and the sinner for whom it was offered. People would lay their hands on the scapegoat, constituting a confession of guilt on the part of the sinner and a transfer of the guilt from the sinner to the victim.

God also said the animals sacrificed were to be without any kind of blemish or mark. The point was that sin (or imperfection) could only be addressed by perfection. Sin cannot reconcile sin. It can only be dealt with by God himself because the sin was against him and his law; therefore, only he can offer true forgiveness. The sacrificial system served as a sign of what God was going to do. It was offered to God, but it wasn't something that would finally and ultimately bridge the gap between us and God. Which is why throughout that time, the great prophets of God said that there would be One who would come—from God—who would take away the sins of the world once and for all. The one sacrifice for all time.

At a point and time in history that God chose for reasons known only to him, God did just that. He provided the perfect, once-for-all sacrifice for the sins of all people throughout all of time and history.

And that brings us to Jesus.

Jesus was the fulfillment of the sacrificial system and, because of him, we can now be forgiven once and for all. The writer of the book of Hebrews in the New Testament likens Jesus to the high priest who went into the Temple on the Day of Atonement on behalf of the people to offer the sacrifice for their sins. Except that this time, instead of the blood of sheep or goats, Jesus offered his own blood. Or, as the man known as John the Baptist said upon seeing Jesus, "Look, the Lamb of God, who takes away the sin of the world" (John 1:29). This sacrifice is where we see God's holiness intersecting with God's love. This is where justice meets mercy. God cannot deal with sin except as his holiness allows it. If he did not punish it, or make adequate satisfaction for it, he would be forgiving it unjustly, which he cannot do. In other words, to simply forgive out of mercy or to redeem with a wave of the hand would cause him to cease to be God. His holiness demanded what sin demands—the just punishment, the death penalty.

So his love had him take our place.

This explains why Jesus, dying on the cross, cried out, "My God, my God, why have you forsaken me?" (Matt. 27:46). When you read that, it may sound as if he cried out to God the Father as if he had been abandoned. And to be sure, the word *forsaken* did literally mean "abandoned." Jesus was saying, "Why have you left me? Why have you turned away? Why have you left me alone here, now?" Interestingly, in one of the few times in all the Bible, it records him saying this in Aramaic, his boyhood tongue—the most personal, intimate language he could use with his Father. So what was going on? Nothing less than the most terrible moment on the cross of all, worse than anything he had gone through physically. He who knew no sin *became* sin. Christians talk about Jesus dying for our sins. That he took our place. That he paid the price for our wrongdoing. What that means is the death of Jesus involved taking the sin of all of humanity upon himself. At the moment of his death, Jesus carried the weight of the sins of the world—past, present, and future. Every rape, every murder, every lie, every betrayal, every adulterous relationship, every act of child abuse. When he died he carried the evil of terrorism and genocide, the Nazi Holocaust, the brutality of ISIS. He shouldered the acts of Adolf Hitler, Charles Manson, Saddam Hussein, and Osama bin Laden . . . and me and you. In a single, blazing, soul-wrenching moment, the sins of the world were placed on him. And he carried their stain, their weight, their pain, their evil, their darkness.

He was the scapegoat.

As if there couldn't be anything worse, at that moment, for the first and only time in all of eternity, the Father had to turn away from him. The community of the Trinity was shattered, and the Son was utterly, terribly, alone as the embodiment of sin itself. It was in the midst of that separation from the Father, that tearing of the Trinity, that impenetrable darkness of sin, that he surrendered his life in sacrifice. So why did he say, "My God, my God, why have you forsaken me?" Was he really expressing hurt that God turned away?

No. He knew this moment would happen. Would it surprise you to find out that he was expressing love and loyalty, allegiance and trust? You see, what many don't know is that Jesus was quoting a verse from the Old Testament of the Bible—specifically, from the twenty-second chapter in the book of Psalms. It may have been that Jesus's intent was to quote all of it because as terrible as this moment was, it was clearly all a part of God's plan. But he physically couldn't complete the psalm—all he could get out was the first line. So what came next in the twenty-second Psalm? Why out of all of the Scriptures did Jesus quote this one on the cross? When you read Psalm 22 and think about who was saying it, in what condition and what situation, it is stunning:

> My God, my God, why have you forsaken me?
> Why are you so far from . . .
> . . . my cries of anguish? . . .
>
> Yet you are enthroned as the Holy One. . . .

But I am a worm and not a man,
    scorned by everyone, despised by the people.
All who see me mock me;
    they hurl insults. . . .

I am poured out like water,
    and all my bones are out of joint.
My heart has turned to wax;
    it has melted within me.
My mouth is dried up like a potsherd,
    and my tongue sticks to the roof of my mouth;
    you lay me in the dust of death.

Dogs surround me,
    a pack of villains encircles me;
    they pierce my hands and my feet.
All my bones are on display;
    people stare and gloat over me.
They divide my clothes among them
    and cast lots for my garment. . . .

I will declare your name to my people;
    in the assembly I will praise you.
You who fear the LORD, praise him!
    All you descendants of Jacob, honor him!
    Revere him, all you descendants of Israel!
For he has not despised or scorned
    the suffering of the afflicted one. . . .

All the ends of the earth
    will remember and turn to the LORD,
and all the families of the nations
    will bow down before him. . . .

Future generations will be told about the Lord.
They will proclaim his righteousness,
    declaring to a people yet unborn:
    He has done it!
        (Ps. 22:1, 3, 6–7, 14–18, 22–24, 27, 30–31)

By the way, if you've ever wondered why Good Friday—the day commemorating the death of Jesus—is called "good," it is because of this moment on the cross. Sin is not good. Death is not good. But what he did for us in our sin, through his death, was good. So this brings us to grace. The best and simplest definition of grace is that which is freely given and totally undeserved. It's getting what you *don't* deserve and not getting what you do. Grace reaches out, in the midst of our sin, and offers forgiveness. Second chances. Yes, salvation. To have what Christ did on the cross applied to your life.

So What Is Grace?

Don't let this drift gently over your imagination. It is too pronounced, too substantive, for that. Let's say you're behind on your mortgage by three, maybe even four payments. You owe thousands and can't possibly make it up. The bank has started foreclosure proceedings and there's nothing you can do. Then, somebody with the power to forgive that debt—to step in and have the bank wipe it clean—does so. You are ecstatic! You couldn't *be* more grateful. But why is that? It's because you knew the situation you were in. You knew what was going to happen. You knew you were going to lose your house.

Apart from grace, each of us is going to lose our life. We're going to face the full penalty for our sin. Our only hope is for a grace-filled, grace-giving God. I usually describe the situation to people this way, because when it was first described to me along these lines, it connected with me. Imagine you are brought to trial for vehicular homicide. You were driving on the road, exceeding the speed limit, and you hit a child on her way home from school. You are brought to trial, the evidence is presented, and from his bench the judge states, "I find you guilty and sentence you to death." But then he does a strange thing. With compassion in his eyes, he gets up from behind his bench, takes off his robe, walks down to where you stand, embraces you, and says, "But I love you. The penalty must be carried out, for I am an honest and good judge, and what you did was wrong and it must be paid for. But I love you and do not want to see your life end this way. Justice must be carried out. So I will go in your place." And then he walks out of the courtroom and toward the electric chair.

That's what Jesus did for you. This is how it's talked about in the Bible:

> We can understand someone dying for a person worth dying for, and we can understand how someone good and noble could inspire us to selfless sacrifice. But God put his love on the line for us by offering his Son in sacrificial death while we were of no use whatever to him. (Rom. 5:7–8 Message)

So what does that grace look like? Feel like? Let's look at one of the more well-known stories surrounding the life of Jesus:

> The teachers of the law and the Pharisees brought in a woman caught in adultery. They made her stand before the group and said to Jesus, "Teacher, this woman was caught in the act of adultery. In the Law Moses commanded us to stone such women. Now what do you say?" . . .
>
> He straightened up and said to them, "Let any one of you who is without sin be the first to throw a stone at her." . . .
>
> At this, those who heard began to go away one at a time . . . until only Jesus was left, with the woman still standing there. Jesus . . . asked her, "Woman, where are they? Has no one condemned you?"
>
> "No one, sir," she said.
>
> "Then neither do I condemn you," Jesus declared. "Go now and leave your life of sin." (John 8:3–5, 7, 9–11)

That is a story of grace. It is first, though, a story of sin and corruption and decadence and judgment. And *then* it is a story of grace. So let's not miss the dark side, or we won't see how amazing grace really is. There was a lot of darkness. First, we have the sin of the people who brought this woman to Jesus. They didn't have to bring her to Jesus, heaping shame and ridicule on her in front of everyone. They didn't care anything about her. They didn't care if she was beaten or stoned, exposed or humiliated. She was nothing to them. They were cruel and unfeeling. They didn't even bother bringing the man she was caught with because they didn't really care about the act at all. They just wanted to trap Jesus. And here was the trap: if Jesus said, "Yes, stone her," then he would have gotten in trouble with the Roman government in power at that time, because only *they* had the authority to exercise capital punishment. He would have also lost his reputation among the people as being a "friend of sinners." But if Jesus said, "*Don't* stone her," then he would have been accused of being light on sin, compromising, and weak—someone who didn't really embrace God's law and holiness. They felt that either way, they *had* him on this. The woman was just a pawn. So there was the conniving, heartless, manipulative sin of the people who brought her before Jesus.

Then there was the sin of the people who caught her in the act. The Bible is very clear that she was, indeed, caught in the act. That language is important because it was the basis by which they were making their legal claim. It meant they had the evidence needed to convict her. In that day, so that suspicious husbands couldn't accuse their wives without reason, the law required testimony from two witnesses who saw the couple together. And not just together, but lying together and clearly having sex. The two witnesses also had to see this at the same time and place. That's a high bar of evidence. So how could you reach that bar? Pretty much only one way: you had to set the couple up. The law also said that if you were to see someone about to sin in that way, it was your responsibility as a caring and compassionate person to say something to them to try to prevent it, which obviously didn't happen. So the witnesses and whoever else was involved in setting her up for the witnesses sinned.

Then you have the sin of the man who was having sex with her. If they were caught in the act, then he was obviously guilty too. But they let him go—he wasn't needed for the trap (but he certainly was part of the darkness).

Finally, we have the sin of the woman herself. And she did sin. Badly. Not just because she had sex with someone she shouldn't have, and was caught in the act, but since the penalty being asked for was stoning, that tells us she was probably engaged to be married and was having sex with someone who was not her fiancé. That was the specified penalty for an engaged person who was unfaithful to their fiancé. Unfaithful wives could also be sentenced to death, but the law did not specify how they should die. Here they say she *had* to be stoned, which tells us she was engaged and sleeping with someone who wasn't her fiancé. That's a nasty betrayal of trust and speaks volumes about not only her outer world, but her inner one as well.

So who deserved to be stoned? Who deserved to die? Who had engaged in heinous, premeditated, purposeful pursuit of sinful behavior before a holy God, holding him in contempt with their behavior?

All of them.

Just like all of us.

So what happened next? Jesus's words to those who brought the woman have become legendary, almost iconic: "Let any one of you who is without sin be the first to throw a stone at her" (John 8:7). Given the darkness of every party involved, we know that no one could throw a stone, because no one was innocent. Then Jesus said that he would not condemn her either. Why?

Jesus didn't see a woman caught in adultery.

He didn't see her just through the lens of her sin.

He saw her through the eyes of grace.

Everyone but Jesus saw a woman caught in adultery. A moral failure. Someone deserving of condemnation and death. But through the extension of grace, Jesus saw a precious child of God.

Someone who was a struggler in life and who had made many, many mistakes, just like everyone else. He also saw someone who could get past the struggles and grow toward the person God intended. Just like he sees in me . . . and, if I can be so bold, just like he sees in you. God's grace is rooted in wild, radical love for us. A love so wild and radical it was sacrificial. Even unto death. Will Campbell, known for his disarmingly earthy approach to spirituality and life, was once asked a critical question: "In ten words or less, what's the Christian message? . . . Let me have it. Ten words." The answer became suddenly clear.

"We're all bastards but God loves us anyway."[1]

In his book *The Ragamuffin Gospel*, Brennan Manning writes,

> When I get honest, I admit I am a bundle of paradoxes. I believe and I doubt, I hope and I get discouraged, I love and I hate, I feel bad about feeling good, I feel guilty about not feeling guilty. I am trusting and suspicious. I am honest and I still play games. Aristotle said I am a rational animal; I say I am an angel with an incredible capacity for beer.[2]

That's me. Is it you? But here's where grace steps in. God knows who you are too. Manning continues:

> If Jesus appeared at your dining room table tonight with knowledge of everything you are and are not, total comprehension of your life story and every skeleton hidden in your closet; if He laid out the real state of your present discipleship with the hidden agenda, the mixed motives, and the dark desires buried in your psyche, you would feel His acceptance and forgiveness.[3]

That isn't all there was to the story of the woman caught in adultery and brought before Jesus. And it's because grace isn't all there was to his message. It was a message with grace *and* truth. This was the defining mark of Jesus's message. As his biographer and (likely) cousin John wrote, Jesus came "full of grace and truth" (John 1:14). So, after saying he would not condemn her he added these words: "Go now and leave your life of sin" (8:11). In essence: "Turn from the life that led you to this moment, because you are not innocent. Turn from it; see it for what it is. You have been rescued from the penalty of your sin; live like it. You're better than this."

To get the message of Jesus, to get grace right, you have to understand that it's not just about grace. It's about grace and truth. They are inextricably intertwined. Jesus accepted her as someone who mattered to him, but never did he affirm the life she had been living. Jesus didn't condemn her for what she did, but he didn't condone what she did either. Personal acceptance was never combined with lifestyle affirmation. Grace and truth went together. Which means Jesus comes to our defense when we're about to get stoned, but he's also the first one to tell us to stop sleeping around. Or stop anything else that is not God's plan for doing life optimally. As psychologist Henry Cloud has written, grace is accepting relationship. Truth is what is real; it describes how things really are. Truth without grace is just judgment. But grace without truth is just deception.[4] Grace is like a Band-Aid— it's meant to be applied to something. And ideally grace is applied to a desire for life change and from that, to sin. Almost every story Jesus told dripped with this one message: if you are far from God, you can come home. And when you do, you'll be met with grace and then challenged with the truth we all so desperately need.

There was a young girl who grew up on a cherry orchard just outside of Traverse City, Michigan. Her parents, who were a bit old-fashioned, tended to overreact to her nose rings, music, and short skirts. They grounded her a few times, and then one night, when her father knocked on her door after an argument to try to reach out to her, she screamed out, "I hate you!" Later that night, she ran away.

She headed for Detroit, a place she had been only once before on a bus trip with her church youth group to watch the Tigers play. Since the papers were filled with lurid details about the gangs, the drugs, and the violence in downtown Detroit, she thought that would be the last place her parents would look for her.

On her second day in the city, she met a man who drove the biggest car she had ever seen. He offered her a ride, bought her lunch, and arranged for her to have a place to stay. He was just so nice. He even gave her some pills to make her feel better than she'd ever felt before. She thought that she had been right all along—her parents had been keeping her from all the fun and from the good life.

That good life went along for a month . . . two months . . . a year. The man with the big car taught her a few things that men like. And since she was underage, men paid a premium for her. Every now and then she thought about her parents back home, but their lives now seemed so boring and plain and old-fashioned that she could hardly believe she grew up there. She had a brief scare when she saw her picture on a billboard with the headline "Have you seen this child?" But now she had blonde hair and, with all the makeup and jewelry she wore, nobody would mistake her for a child.

After a year, the first signs of the illness began to appear. It amazed her how fast her boss turned mean. He told her that he couldn't risk having anyone around who was sick like that, and he threw her out on the street without a penny to her name.

She found that she was able to turn a couple of tricks a night, but they didn't pay much, and all the money went to support her drug habit. When winter came, she found herself sleeping on metal grates outside the large downtown department stores. *Sleeping* is the wrong word, though. A teenage girl at night in downtown Detroit can never relax her guard. Soon dark bands circled her eyes and her cough worsened.

One night, as she lay awake listening for footsteps that might harm her, everything about her life suddenly looked different. She felt, for the first time in a year, like the little girl that she was, lost in a cold and frightening city. She began to cry. Her pockets were empty and she was hungry. She needed a fix. She pulled her legs underneath her and shivered under the newspapers she'd piled on top of her coat trying to stay warm. Suddenly a memory came into her mind of May and springtime in her hometown, with a million cherry trees in bloom and her golden retriever chasing a tennis ball. And she said to herself, "Oh God, why did I leave?" And she started to cry again and knew that more than anything else in the world she wanted to go home. So she tried to call her parents.

Three straight calls, three straight connections to voicemail. But on the third one, she finally left a message. "Dad, Mom, it's me. I was wondering about maybe coming home. I'm catching a bus up your way, and it'll get there about midnight tomorrow. If you're not there, I get it. I guess I'll just stay on the bus."

It took about seven hours for a bus to make all the stops between Detroit and her home, and during that time all she could think about were the flaws in her plan. What if they were out of town and didn't get the message? What if they were home, but. she didn't give them enough time to be at the bus station? What if they didn't even want her back?

Then she began to rehearse what she would say:

"Dad, I'm so sorry. I know I was wrong. It's not your fault—it's all mine. Dad, can you forgive me?" She said the words over and over, practicing.

When the bus finally rolled into the station, the driver said, "Traverse City, Michigan. Fifteen-minute stop." Fifteen minutes for her entire life to be decided. She checked herself in a compact mirror, smoothed her hair, licked the lipstick off her teeth. She looked at the tobacco stains on her fingertips and wondered if her parents would notice. *If* they were even there.

She got off the bus and walked into the terminal, not knowing what to expect. But not one of a thousand scenes that entered her mind matched what she saw. Because there, within those concrete walls and plastic chairs in that bus terminal, stood a group of forty brothers and sisters, great-aunts and uncles and cousins, a grandmother and even a great-grandmother. They were all wearing goofy

The Return of the Prodigal Son, painted by Rembrandt c. 1669

party hats and blowing noisemakers, and taped across the entire wall of the terminal was a banner that read, "Welcome home!"

Then out of the crowd stepped her dad. Through tears, she started to say, "Dad, I'm sorry. I know . . ." And he stopped her. "Hush, child. We've got no time for that. You'll be late for the party. A banquet's waiting for you at home."[5]

That story is a retelling of a story Jesus told, a story often referred to as the story of the prodigal son. A story that, in one form or another, he told over and over again. A story of someone who turned away from God, found out that it wasn't the life they wanted, came back . . . and found out they could.

But Can There Really Be Just One Way?

You walk into a Starbucks, and you order a tall, half-caf soy latte at 120 degrees. Or a triple, venti, half-sweet, nonfat caramel macchiato. Or a grande, quad, nonfat, one-pump, no-whip mocha. Or if you're me, you just say, "Caffeine, please!" According to Starbucks' Global Chief Marketing Officer, there are now more than 80,000 different ways you can order a Starbucks coffee.[6] When John Naisbitt wrote his prescient book *Megatrends* back in the '80s, he said that one of the top ten trends of the modern world would be a shift from no choice to multiple choices. And he was right. We've come to expect it. It's just the way things are.

But what about God? Can't grace and truth be found in other places? Isn't there more than just one way to come home? When it comes to an authoritative spiritual text, there's the Bible, the Bhagavad Gita, the Koran, and the Book of Mormon. When it comes to religious leaders, you can select from Krishna, Buddha, and Mohammed. When it comes to religious groups, you can link up with those in Islam, Hinduism, Buddhism, Judaism, or Scientology. No wonder it's almost natural to believe that searching for God is like climbing a mountain. Since everyone knows that there is not just *one* way to climb a mountain—mountains are way too big for that—there must be any number of paths that can be taken. We tend to look at all of the ideas about God throughout all the religions of the world as just different ways up the mountain. So where does that leave you? You're free to choose! Take your pick from among the countless philosophies and worldviews littering the cultural landscape. Why? Because all roads lead to God. All spiritual paths are equally legitimate. It doesn't really matter what you believe, much less who, what, or how you worship.

The only problem is that there's one faith that isn't playing well in this sandbox, and it happens to be the Christian faith. Jesus spoke directly to this idea and had some provocative words to say: "I am the way and the truth and the life. No one comes to the Father except through me" (John 14:6). In that statement, Jesus makes it clear that there *is* a Father God and that there's only one way *to* that Father God—through him. And he was very careful with his language in that verse. Jesus didn't say that he was *a* way, or *a* truth, but *the* way, *the* truth, and *the* life. And that no one—*no one*—can enter into a full relationship with God apart from him. That was as politically incorrect then as it is now, but it has marked Christianity from its beginning. "It is by the name of Jesus Christ," the apostle and early Christian leader Peter declared; "salvation is found in no one else, for there is no other name given under heaven by which we must be saved" (Acts 4:10, 12 TNIV).

For a lot of people, that just makes them cringe. You may be among them. The idea that Christianity, and specifically Jesus, is the only way to God is so out of sync with the way we think. Beginning with its dismissal of other ways to God. That seems too . . . well . . . dismissive. Is Christianity saying that every other religion is just completely wrong? Actually, no. C. S. Lewis once wrote, "If you are a Christian you do not have to believe that all the other religions are simply wrong all through. . . . If you are a Christian, you are free to think that all these religions, even the queerest ones, might contain at least some hint of the truth."[7]

Wikimedia Commons

A photo of Tian Tan Buddha, also known as "Big Buddha," on Lantau Island, Hong Kong

Lewis goes on to suggest we think of it in terms of arithmetic. There is one and only one right answer to 2 + 2—and that's 4— but if you were to answer 6 it would be a lot closer than answering 37. While there is only one right answer, some answers are closer to being right than others.

That's not all. If all truth is God's truth, then it remains truth wherever we find it. So as a Christian, I can appreciate the truth in much of Buddhism's ideas, such as the first two of the Four Noble Truths that state there is a lot of suffering in the world (obviously), and that our desires are often at the root of that suffering. Buddhism also teaches many things that I can appreciate and affirm as clearly moral: you shouldn't engage in murder, you shouldn't steal, you shouldn't engage in immoral sexual behavior, and you shouldn't lie.

But just because there may be goodness and truth in other places doesn't mean you have also found an equally legitimate way to God. In fact, the full teaching of that religion may involve a road that is heading in the totally opposite direction. Let's stick with the example of Buddhism. While there is some common ground between Buddhism and Christianity, there are also enormous tension points. The Dalai Lama himself has stated publicly that the central doctrines of Buddhism and Christianity are not compatible. He has been quite open with the fact that you cannot be a Buddhist Christian, or a Christian Buddhist. And he is right. Christianity believes in a personal God; Buddhism does not even believe in a Higher Being (Buddhism is, essentially, an atheistic religion). That is a divide that is simply insurmountable. That's not two different ways up the same mountain; those are different places on the map.

This is true when you compare Christianity to the other major world religions as well: Christians believe there's one God; Hindus believe there are millions. Christians embrace Jesus as God himself in human form; Muslims don't even rank Jesus at the top of the prophets, much less the Savior of the world. When you have divisions like this, you have only two options. You can either say that somebody is right in that particular area and everybody else is wrong, or you can say that everyone is wrong. What you can't say is that everyone is right—that it's all the same path, the same idea, the same God. That would be intellectually confused at best and intellectually dishonest at worst. And the areas of disagreement are not trivial in nature. They deal with the very existence of God and, if he does exist, how we enter into a relationship with this God (not to mention the identity of a person like Jesus).

Right about now you may be thinking, *Okay, let me add this up. You're saying that there is just one way to God and it's through Jesus. And while there may be some truth or good in other religions, that doesn't mean they are equally valid ways to God. So . . . are you saying that all non-Christian people just wind up in hell? That someone really good, really noble, like Gandhi, is in hell just because he wasn't a Christian? Because if you are, you've lost me. I just can't believe that's right.* Fair enough. But now let me see if I can add up what *you're* saying: all that should matter, in the end, is how good you are. Everyone should be banking on some kind of "goodness quotient." And since we define goodness

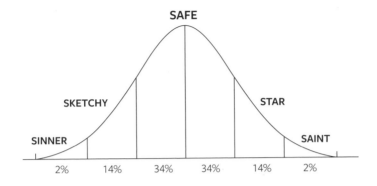

in relation to other people, what you're saying is God should grade on a cosmic curve. And if God doesn't grade on a curve, you're not sure you can believe in that God.

Just for fun, let's remember what grading on a curve is about. It's when grading is relative. On any given assignment, your grade is based on the performance of the class as a whole. So if everybody does poorly but you make a 75 percent, and that 75 percent is the highest grade in the class, instead of a C suddenly you've got an A. Because on a curve, the highest grade, no matter how bad it is, is given the equivalent of a 100 percent—an A. Even though you made a 75 percent, because you did better than everybody else, you get an A. It gets better. Whatever the average grade is becomes the average grade. So if the average is 40, instead of an F, that's a C.

We like getting graded on a curve. Particularly because we come out looking better, feeling better, and doing better than we deserve. So what might that look like if we were to apply that to spiritual things?

The 2 percent on either side is easy. On the **Sinner** side are the Hitlers, the bin Ladens, the rapists and pedophiles, telemarketers, and spam senders. We know who's over there. On the **Saint** side is Mother Teresa or Gandhi. So those are your F and A grades. Now let's talk about the Ds. These are the people who are, at best, **Sketchy**. They aren't the darkest of the dark, but they are far from

Boy Scouts. These are people who lie, cheat, steal. So here we're talking car salesmen and members of Congress. Before you think that's a joke, according to a Gallup poll, those really are the two least trusted professions in the United States.[8]

Now for the 14 percent with the B grades. These are the people who are above average in their goodness. They set the day-in, day-out standard for most of us in terms of virtue or spiritual commitment. They are our role models and heroes. They are our celebrities, our **Stars**. Medical missionaries, like those who risked their lives serving Ebola patients. Christian leaders like the late Billy Graham. Throw in a few pastors and social workers.

So where does that leave most people within the typical bell curve? Those in the C-, C, and C+ range? Which, in our "grading on a curve" minds, means **Safe**? Not saints, but not sinners. Not a star, but not sketchy either. In other words, me and you. So we're okay. We're safe. Any other scale makes us nervous and insecure, so we reject it.

But what if that's not how God grades? What if the bell curve is all wrong and we're not graded on a curve at all? What if the whole thing doesn't even involve a letter grade? What if it is . . . pass/fail?

You're in or you're out. You're through or you're gone. You say, "Well, I don't know if I like that." Well, I don't imagine that any of us do. It's scary stuff to think about. But in full transparency, let me give you a headline: that's what the Bible teaches. The Bible only talks about pass/fail; it doesn't mention anything about a curve. And here's where it gets even worse: we aren't even graded based on a graduated scale at all, but on a person. And that person is God himself. In other words, everything on this pass/fail scale has to do with whether you are as good as God.

So what's going on? The truth is that none of us are okay—not even one. None of us are "good" enough to earn salvation. As Joseph de Maistre once observed, "I do not know what the heart of the rascal may be; I know what is in the heart of an honest man;

it is horrible."[9] No one is in less of a broken relationship with God, and in less need of the *way* to God, than anyone else. And that's the real issue: how to be made right with God. Every human being is in a broken relationship with God through the sin in their life. The only way to repair that relationship is to become reconciled with God himself. The God of the Bible has said that there is one and only one way for that to happen—one and only one way to have your sins against him forgiven. The way he provided, which is through what Jesus did on the cross. Jesus's death on the cross was the payment for our sins. The only payment that was ever made.

And that's what makes Jesus the only way.

Now, as I've already acknowledged, there are many visceral reactions against this idea, not the least of which has to do with sincerity. That it isn't *what* you believe that matters, but *how* you believe. Something deep inside of us knows, and I think correctly, that the nature of true spirituality is somehow connected with *authenticity*. This is why people like Mother Teresa and Nelson Mandela—both Christians—were so widely respected by Christians and non-Christians alike. But it is one thing to value sincerity and another to make sincerity the lone characteristic of spiritual truth, much less spiritual standing. *How* you believe matters, but so does *what* you believe. If you say that it doesn't matter what you believe as long as you are sincere, you miss a very important point. You can be sincerely *wrong*. I can sincerely believe that when I reach into my medicine cabinet at 3:00 a.m. with a headache that I am taking an aspirin, but if I am really taking cyanide my sincerity will not save me from the perils of the poison I've ingested into my system. If I put carbolic acid into my eyes instead of contact lens solution, no matter how sincerely I believe I've grabbed the right bottle, I will still do damage to my vision. During World War II, Adolf Hitler *sincerely believed* that the slaughter of six million Jews was justified, but he was *sincerely wrong*. Sincerity matters, but it cannot be *all* that matters, because sincerity alone

Wikimedia Commons; Photo Credit: David R. Tribble

Photo of Penn Jillette at the Rio Hotel in Las Vegas

cannot alter physical, much less moral, reality. So it is not simply the sincerity of our faith that matters, but the *object* of our faith. Faith is very much like a rope—it matters what you tie it to.

Another visceral concern has to do with spiritual hubris, the idea that no religion should think it is better than another religion. Yes, you might believe you adhere to the truth, but that would be arrogant to assume, so the best thing to do is to function like an agnostic. And by all means, don't try to convince others of your convictions. But is it really arrogant to tell others about what you believe is true, or is it compassion?

Penn Jillette is the "talkative" half of Penn and Teller, the Las Vegas comedy-illusion team. Penn has been an outspoken atheist. But Christians can learn a lot from a video blog he posted on his personal website that talks about a man who gave him a Bible:

> At the end of the show as I've mentioned before, we go out and we talk to folks, you know, sign an occasional autograph and shake hands and so on. And there was one guy waiting over to the side in the, uh, what I call the "hover position" after it was all done. . . . He had been the guy who picks the joke during our psychic comedian section of the show. So he had the props from that in his hand because we give those away—the joke book, the envelope, and the paper, and stuff. . . .
>
> And he walked over to me and he said, "I was here last night at the show, and I saw the show and I liked the show. . . ." He was very complimentary about my use of language and complimentary about honesty and stuff. He said nice stuff, no need to go into it, he said nice stuff.

And then he said, "I brought this for you," and he handed me a Gideon pocket edition. I thought it said from the New Testament but also, Psalms is from the New Testament, right? Little book. . . . And he said, "I wrote in the front of it and I wanted you to have this. I'm kind of proselytizing." And then he said, "I'm a businessman. I'm sane, I'm not crazy." And he looked me right in the eye and did all of this. And it was really wonderful.

I believe he knew that I was an atheist. But he was not defensive. And he looked me right in the eyes. And he was truly complimentary . . . it didn't seem like empty flattery. He was really kind and nice and sane and looked me in the eyes and talked to me and then gave me this Bible. And I've always said, you know, that I don't respect people who don't proselytize. I don't respect that at all. If you believe that there's a heaven and hell and that people could be going to hell or not getting eternal life or whatever, and you think that, well, it's not really worth telling them this because it would make it socially awkward. . . . How much do you have to hate somebody to not proselytize? How much do you have to hate somebody to believe that everlasting life is possible and not tell them that?

I mean, if I believed beyond a shadow of a doubt that a truck was coming at you and you didn't believe it, but that truck was bearing down on you, there's a certain point where I tackle you. And this is more important than that. And I've always thought that and I've written about that and I've thought of it conceptually.

This guy was a really good guy. He was polite, and honest, and sane and he cared enough about me to proselytize and give me a Bible. Which had written in it a little note to me . . . just like, liked your show and so on. And then like five phone numbers for him and an email address if I wanted to get in touch. Now, I know there's no God. And one polite person living his life right doesn't change that. But I'll tell ya, he was a very, very, very good man. And that's real important. And with that kind of goodness it's okay to have that deep of a disagreement. I still think that religion does a lot of bad stuff. But man, that was a good man who gave me that book. That's all I wanted to say.[10]

That line rings so true: If I believe where you stand with Christ will determine your entire eternal trajectory, how much would I have to hate you to not make my convictions known? Ultimately, the question is whether we believe that truth even exists. Historically, the most common idea of truth is the correspondence between our ideas or perceptions and reality.[11] That's why it's called the "correspondence theory of truth." If I make the statement, "It is raining," it is only true if I look outside and find that it is raining. What is true is that which actually *is*.[12] The belief in more than one way to God is really a belief that truth does not exist or, even more to the point, that truth doesn't matter. But it does. Even a skeptic as noteworthy as Sigmund Freud maintained that if "it were really a matter of indifference what we believed, then we might just as well build our bridges of cardboard as of stone, or inject a tenth of a gramme of morphia into a patient instead of a hundredth, or take tear-gas as a narcotic instead of ether."[13]

Let's get back to the Gandhi question. If Christianity is the only way, then does that mean that God is going to send everyone else to hell? Before we address that directly, in light of the "grading on a curve" dynamic, it's important to understand that the Bible teaches that it isn't God's desire that *anyone* should experience hell as a punishment for their broken relationship with him, but that everyone would receive the gift of eternal life in heaven through Christ. But since God didn't make us mindless robots, we have a free choice to accept that gift or reject that gift, and there are consequences that come with our freedom to choose or else the choice would be meaningless. Ready for the big reveal? God doesn't send anyone to hell. We choose our own destination of our own free will. This is how the Bible puts it: "Whoever believes in him [Jesus] is not condemned, but whoever does not believe stands condemned already because they have not believed. . . . This is the verdict: Light has come into the world, but men loved darkness instead" (John 3:18–19). And it's the same with the person who has chosen to embrace the Christian faith. The judgment of

God will simply affirm the decision that has already been made. This is how Jesus phrased it: "Very truly I tell you, whoever hears my word and believes him who sent me has eternal life and will not be judged but has crossed over from death to life" (John 5:24).

So when someone asks, "How can a loving God send someone to hell?" the answer often surprises: "He doesn't. We send ourselves." Think of it this way. Imagine you are out at sea and your boat begins to sink. You are clinging to a life raft in the middle of the ocean. A boat finds you and comes to you and offers to pull you to safety from your raft. You can either let yourself be saved or allow yourself to die. If you refuse their help, they aren't sending you to a death at sea. *You* are sending yourself.

Wikimedia Commons

Mahatma Gandhi in Delhi, India, 1946

Hell exists because of our decisions and we send ourselves. The life and death of Jesus was about what God was willing to do to save people from the consequences of those decisions. But we have to take him up on the offer. If not, then yes, hell is inevitable. So is Gandhi in hell? The most direct answer is that Gandhi is where Gandhi chose to be. And that's how the final judgment will work. God will do the right and just thing by everyone. He will make the just judgment. Whatever the verdict is on anyone's life, it will be right and good. We will go where we decided, to the last dying breath of our life, to go. As C. S. Lewis once observed, we can bend a knee toward God in this life and say, "Thy will be done." Or, at the end of our life, force God to say to us, "*Thy* will be done."[14]

Now, some might push back and say, "But why is there even a hell? That doesn't sound like a loving God. Why would a loving God have something like hell in existence?"

I *totally* disagree.

The existence of heaven and hell shows that this is a moral universe, that God is a moral God, and that there is truth and justice and righteousness. Do you really want a spiritual universe, a moral order, without hell? Without punishment? Where Hitler and bin Laden are as rewarded as Mother Teresa? Do you want a cosmic order where pedophiles are praised and rapists are celebrated? Where nothing is seen as sin? A God that just kind of chuckles at it all in some kind of stupid senility? Is that what you think is good and right? I get that hell is disturbing to you. It should be disturbing to you. It's disturbing to me. Deeply disturbing. It should be a hard-edged truth. But it's a truth. A necessary truth. There wouldn't be a moral universe without it. Hell is a terrible, dreadful, horrific place, but its existence isn't what is evil. Its existence is what is moral.

With that in mind, you might be wondering about those who have never heard about Jesus or who don't have the mental ability to understand. This is a heartbreaking question because you might have in mind infants or very young children who may have died before having any ability to know or to "hear" about Jesus, much less to respond. Or, perhaps, people with special needs or cognitive challenges that make truly understanding and embracing all of this nearly impossible. As tragic and heartbreaking as the question is, the answer is very simple: ultimately, this is answered in and through the very character of God. What I mean by that is either God is a good God, a just God, a fair God . . . or he's not. If he is, then he'll do the right thing by everyone, based on their ability to hear and understand and respond. So when someone asks if their baby who died is in heaven, I can say, "That is the one thing that you don't need to be worrying about in this moment. Your child is being cradled, right now, in the arms of God. Absolutely they are in heaven." Why can I say that?

Because we have a good God.

And what about those people in parts of the world who have never even heard about Jesus? Someone who was never told about Jesus? That's a little different. They are still held accountable based on the knowledge available to them through what can be seen through what has been made. Here's how it's talked about in the Bible:

> But God shows his anger from heaven against all sinful, wicked people who suppress the truth by their wickedness. They know the truth about God because he has made it obvious to them. For ever since the world was created, people have seen the earth and sky. Through everything God made, they can clearly see his invisible qualities—his eternal power and divine nature. So they have no excuse for not knowing God.
>
> Yes, they knew God, but they wouldn't worship him as God or even give him thanks. And they began to think up foolish ideas of what God was like. As a result, their minds became dark and confused. Claiming to be wise, they instead became utter fools. And instead of worshiping the glorious, ever-living God, they worshiped idols made to look like mere people and birds and animals and reptiles. (Rom. 1:18–23 NLT)

Each of us is held accountable by the raw wonder of creation all around us that is so intricate in its design that it begs for the notion of a Creator God. So how could this work positively in someone's life? Imagine in the darkest recesses of a rainforest, a man is walking along one day and comes upon a tree stump that has died and is rotting. He walks over to it and sees that it's filled with water. He gazes at his reflection for a few moments and he thinks, *You know . . . I didn't make me. And that totem carving we've been worshiping and praying to has never done anything for me. It just seems to be nothing more than any other dead tree.* And then he gazes at the sky and the stars and says, "Whoever you are, whatever you are, help! I want to know . . . you."

Does God hear that prayer?

Of course.

As C. S. Lewis remarked, "We do know that no man can be saved except through Christ; we do not know that only those who know him can be saved through him."[15] This does not mean that people will be saved by Christ through the channel of other religions, but simply that all persons will be judged fairly by God on the basis of their *knowledge* of Christ and their ability to *respond* to that knowledge. So while Christians believe that choices have consequences, and hell is real, no one *has* to go there. *The* way, *the* truth, and *the* life is available to us all.

5

THE BOOK

The problem of reading the Holy Book—if you have faith it is the Word of God—is the most difficult problem in the whole field of reading. . . . The Word of God is obviously the most difficult writing men can read; but it is also, if you believe it is the Word of God, the most important to read.

Mortimer Adler, *How to Read a Book*, 1972

Every year Stephen Prothero, chairman of the religion department of Boston University, gives his undergraduate students a fifteen-question quiz.

And every year they fail.

And it's all about the Bible.

Want to give it a try? I won't put you through the whole test—let's just dip in and out of a few of the questions to see if you know the answers. Here we go:

1. Name the Four Gospels.

2. Where according to the Bible was Jesus born?

3. President George W. Bush spoke in his first inaugural address of the Jericho road. What Bible story was he invoking?

4. What are the first five books of the Hebrew Bible or the Christian Old Testament?

5. What is the Golden Rule?

6. "God helps those who help themselves." Is this in the Bible? If so, where?

7. "Blessed are the poor in spirit, for theirs is the kingdom of God." Does this appear in the Bible?

8. Name the Ten Commandments.[1]

So how did you do? Let's find out.

1. Name the Four Gospels.
   Answer: Matthew, Mark, Luke, John

2. Where according to the Bible was Jesus born?
   Answer: Bethlehem

3. President George W. Bush spoke in his first inaugural address of the Jericho road. What Bible story was he invoking?
   Answer: The Good Samaritan

4. What are the first five books of the Hebrew Bible or the Christian Old Testament?
   Answer: Genesis, Exodus, Leviticus, Numbers, Deuteronomy

5. What is the Golden Rule?
   Answer: "Do unto others as you would have them do unto you" (see Matt. 7:12).

6. "God helps those who help themselves." Is this in the Bible? If so, where?
   Answer: No, this is not in the Bible. The words are Benjamin Franklin's.

7. "Blessed are the poor in spirit, for theirs is the kingdom of God." Does this appear in the Bible?
   Answer: Yes, in the Beatitudes of Jesus's Sermon on the Mount (Matt. 5:3).

8. Name the Ten Commandments.
   Answer: No other gods before me;
   You shall not make yourself a graven image;
   You shall not take the name of the Lord in vain;
   Remember the Sabbath and keep it holy;
   Honor your father and mother;
   You shall not murder;
   You shall not commit adultery;
   You shall not steal;
   You shall not bear false witness against your neighbor;
   You shall not covet.

Now, why does he give that test every year? He says it's because everybody should know the basics of the Bible. In fact, in a commentary for the *Los Angeles Times* titled "We Live in the Land of Biblical Idiots," Prothero, who grew up Episcopalian and then became (in his own words) a "spiritually confused Christian," was one of those idiots! And knew he shouldn't be. So what should you know about the Bible?

Four things.

The Bible Is a Library

First, the Bible is a library. It isn't a single book; it is a collection of books. Sixty-six books, to be exact, written by more than forty authors and covering a period of around fifteen hundred years. Most of the books bear the name of their author and are straightforward. The book of Isaiah was the book written by Isaiah, the book of Daniel was the book written by Daniel. Sometimes, the books carry the name of the main event that the book talks about. For example, the book of Genesis is about the genesis—the creation, the beginning—of the world. The book of Exodus deals mostly with the great exodus, or departure, of the Jewish people from slavery under the leadership of Moses. Some of the books are actually letters and carry the name of the people they were sent to. So Philippians is the name of the book, or letter, sent to the people who lived in the city of Philippi. First and 2 Corinthians are the two letters sent to the people who lived in Corinth. First and 2 Timothy are two letters a man named Paul sent to a man he was mentoring named Timothy. So the Bible is a library of books, reflecting different times in history, different authors, different settings, and different emphases.

The Bible Has Two Testaments

The second big headline is that this library of books falls into two parts, usually called "testaments"—the Old Testament and the New Testament. The Old Testament is made up of thirty-nine of the sixty-six books, and the New Testament is made up of twenty-seven of the sixty-six books.

The word *testament* simply means "agreement" or "covenant." It refers to a pact, a treaty, an alliance, an agreement between two parties. And that tells you something about the content of the Bible. The Bible is a record of God's great covenants, his promises, with us in regard to our relationship with him. It's a record of God's dealings with us. The Old Testament is a record of God's agreements with people *before* the time of Jesus. The New Testament covers everything that happened *when* Jesus came and then what happened after his resurrection.

So if you want to know what divides the Old Testament from the New Testament, it's Jesus. Jesus is the One who separates the two sections of Scripture. Jesus's coming altered all of history, and all talk of sacred Scripture is about that which came before Christ and that which came after Christ. The Old Testament builds toward the New Testament; it looks forward to the New Testament. And then the New Testament fulfills the Old Testament and completes it; it's as if it writes the final chapters to the story, always looking back to the foreword.

If you like *The Lord of the Rings* trilogy, you can think of the Old Testament as *The Fellowship of the Ring* followed by *The Two Towers* (the Old Testament takes two films because it has the most books), and then the New Testament is like the final installment, *The Return of the King.*

If you don't like *The Lord of the Rings*, forget I said any of that. But like *The Lord of the Rings*, everything in the Bible *is* about the King. Only his name is Jesus, not Aragorn. The Old Testament looks forward to the coming of Jesus and the New Testament looks back on his coming. So while the Bible is sixty-six books, in two parts, it's still one story. That's why it's called the Bible. The English word *Bible* comes from the name of the papyrus, or "byblos" reed, that was used for making scrolls and books. Because they were made from byblos reeds, books came to be known as bibles. But the writings of the Old Testament and the New Testament were so sacred, so special, so revered, that they came to be known simply as *the* book, or *the* Bible.

The Bible Is Sacred

But why are these considered the sacred writings? Why these sixty-six books and not others? Why are these considered the Word of God? That's our third headline. Christians take the writings of the Bible as the Word of God for our lives for one reason: Jesus. Yes, the Old Testament was seen as sacred before Jesus—those books recorded God's dealings and God's prophets, who people saw and heard. And the same with the New Testament. But Jesus is the

One who brings confirmation to both testaments. Here's why: if you believe Jesus was who he said he was—God himself in human form—then what he said is what matters more than anything. So if he said something was Scripture, or he set in motion the writing of something to *be* Scripture, then it *is* Scripture. If he was who he said he was, then it's not about what books I think ought to be set apart as sacred or inspired, or what books you think should make the cut, but what *he* said about it.

And the Bible we have is the one he set apart.

Let's unpack that a bit. First, we accept the Old Testament as Scripture because Jesus did. When Jesus made reference to the Scriptures, he was referring to the Old Testament we have today. When the New Testament records Jesus saying he believed in the Scriptures, that meant the Old Testament, because the New Testament had not been written yet. And here was his unqualified endorsement: "For truly I tell you, until heaven and earth disappear, not the smallest letter, not the least stroke of a pen, will by any means disappear from the Law [of Moses] until everything is accomplished" (Matt. 5:18). And then he also said, "[The] Scripture cannot be set aside" (John 10:35). In what may be one of the most intriguing statements he made in relation to the Old Testament, Jesus introduced a quote from the Old Testament by saying, "David himself, speaking by the Holy Spirit, declared . . ." (Mark 12:36) and then went on to quote what David said in the Old Testament book of Psalms. Clearly, to Jesus, the Old Testament was no ordinary collection of writings. He referred to the writers of the Old Testament as being inspired by the Holy Spirit, thus giving us the very Word of God.

When we come to the New Testament, again, we look to Jesus to give it authority. And he did. Much of the New Testament records what he said and taught. And if he was God in human form and said something, I would call that Scripture! But he also laid the foundation for the writings of the rest of the New Testament to be accepted as Scripture through the apostles. Jesus chose the word *apostle* for a very small, very select group of his disciples in order to indicate their unique role. The word *apostle* means "those who have been sent," and the mission Jesus sent them on was that of preaching and teaching. The word is used only of the twelve originally chosen by Jesus and a handful of select others, most notably the apostle Paul. The apostles received a unique commission from Jesus himself, never to be repeated, to assume a prophetic role and speak God's word to the people. Apostles were never self-appointed. The most literal translation of the Greek language has Jesus saying to Paul in the book of Acts, chapter 26, "I apostle you." Each was then given a historical experience of interaction with Jesus himself. They spent time with Jesus and were mentored by Jesus. This is why when a replacement was selected for Judas the principal requirement was that the person be someone who had been with Jesus throughout his ministry so they could be a true eyewitness and direct bearer of the teaching of Jesus. For Paul, the last apostle appointed, it was a post-resurrection interaction and appointment. Without this, he could not have been an apostle. These were the men who were to speak in Jesus's name and carry his word to others. They carried the very authority of Jesus himself as they taught. Jesus even said these words to them: "Anyone who welcomes you, welcomes me" (Matt. 10:40).

Each apostle was given a special inspiration for their teaching from Jesus himself through the Holy Spirit. While all Christians have the Holy Spirit operating within them from the moment of their decision to become a Christ follower, Jesus promised the apostles a special ministry of the Holy Spirit in regard to their teaching and writing. The Holy Spirit gave them a remembrance of the teaching of Jesus and inspired them to teach other truths from God as well. Jesus also said that they would be guided into all truth: "The Spirit shows what is true and will come and guide you into the full truth . . . by taking my message and telling it to you" (John 16:13–14 CEV).

CHRISTIANITY FOR PEOPLE WHO AREN'T CHRISTIANS

This is why the teachings of the apostles were considered Scripture, and the mark of what would be included in the New Testament was simple: Was it written by, or based on, the teaching of Jesus or one of his apostles? This is why we read in the book of Acts, which records the history of the early church and the "acts" of the apostles, these words: "[the early church] devoted themselves to the apostles' teaching" (Acts 2:42). Why? Because they knew exactly what Jesus had done—they saw and heard Jesus appoint them! They saw and heard Jesus teach on the kind of role the apostles were going to have. They knew that Peter and John, James and Paul were not, in this sense, ordinary men. The teaching of the apostles was the teaching of Christ. To receive them was to receive Christ; to reject them was to reject Christ.

So when it comes to the Bible, we didn't choose these books. It wasn't something a group of church leaders sat down one day and randomly picked. Jesus had already embraced and affirmed the Old Testament as the Word of God; the first four books of the New Testament capture his own life and teaching as God himself in human form come to earth; the rest of the New Testament was personally commissioned by Jesus, written by his chosen apostles through a special working of the Holy Spirit as they wrote. This is why, when the ancient church made the Old Testament official through the Council of Jamnia in AD 90 and the New Testament official in AD 397 through the Council of Carthage, it wasn't a selection process. It was simply a formal recognition of what had already been established.

For the Christian, that's our Bible. This is what God wanted us to know. Of course, you are welcome to reject Jesus and to reject the Bible. But what you can't do is accept Jesus and then reject the Bible, because he's the one who set it apart. It would be a little weird to say, "Jesus, I've come to you for my eternity, to save me from my sins. I'm banking all of eternity on you and I believe you are God himself in human form who came to earth. I believe that you did miracles and you died for my sins and rose from the dead. But this book of yours, I can't buy into it. I don't believe that you have the power to set aside a collection of writings for your followers. So while I believe everything else, I think you're completely untrustworthy when it comes to this."

No.

You're welcome to reject Jesus and reject the Bible. But what you can't do is accept Jesus and reject the Bible. He didn't give you that option. Jesus tells us it is God's revelation to us. The word *revelation* comes from the Latin word *revelatio* that means to "draw back the curtain." It was a theater term. Imagine a stage where a play is about to begin. You can't know the story until the curtain is pulled back, until it's revealed. That's the Bible—God's revelation. It's God revealing himself and truth about himself that could not otherwise be known.

So, what about all of those "lost" books of the Bible you've heard about? No one denies the existence of other ancient writings within the first five centuries following the life of Jesus. No one denies that some of them contain things that go against the Gospels and their eyewitness accounts. No one denies that there are documents with names such as the "Gospel of Mary Magdalene," or the "Gospel of Thomas," or even the "Gospel of Judas Iscariot." That's not news. Not now, and not then.

But even then, they were uniformly understood to be forgeries, false in their information and most written two hundred to three hundred years after the time their alleged authors lived. And what they claimed went against everything the eyewitnesses of the early Christian movement knew to be true. For example, what is called the "Gospel of Mary" denies the resurrection, argues against a second coming of Christ, and rejects the suffering and death of Jesus as a path to eternal life. The manuscript even claims that Jesus said there is no such thing as sin. That's why this writing, and others like it, never took hold. Even the ones that appeared right after the life and death of Jesus. People at the time knew that they were diametrically opposed to what Jesus actually said and, since they were present when he said it, they were never taken seriously. It was clear that they were obvious attempts to undermine the integrity of the actual records of Jesus's life and teaching. The fact that such a document surfaces again in our day through archaeology does not mean we should give it any more credence than they gave it back then.

Let's say that I wrote a book about the 2018 Super Bowl between the Philadelphia Eagles and the New England Patriots. But, instead of writing that the Eagles beat the Patriots by the score of 41–33, which we know is what happened, let's imagine that I claim that my beloved Carolina Panthers stormed their way to the big game and beat the Eagles 34–3 the way I'm sure God originally intended. And let's say that in my book, I cite all kinds of made-up statistics and play-by-play analysis, and then self-publish it as an ebook on Amazon as an actual record of what took place. My goal? To change people's minds about who won because I am

Carolina Panthers at Bank of America Stadium (Panthers' home stadium) in Charlotte, NC

anti-Philly. Would anybody buy it, unless as a joke book for a Panthers fan? Would anybody actually believe it as historical record? Of course not. If intended to be a credible account of the 52nd Super Bowl, it would swiftly be denounced and become culturally irrelevant. Why? Because more than 100 million people watched the game. But let's say a printed copy of this book finds its way to a garbage dump and it gets buried, and three hundred years from now people find it. They look at it and they say, "Whoa, people back then did not believe the Eagles won! There's an alternate view. The Panthers might have won the 52nd Super Bowl. Look, it's right here! And it's three hundred years old! Why, it's as old as the official NFL records we have!" Yeah, but we also know that it's a three-hundred-year-old piece of . . . well, you know. And it was considered as much back then.

This is why the early biographies on the life and teaching and ministry of Jesus, written by those who were eyewitnesses to his life and teaching, took hold. When the earliest accounts written by Matthew, Mark, Luke, and John came out, people were still around who had seen and heard Jesus. They knew whether what was said in the Gospels actually happened. And they weren't rejected. Instead, they ignited a movement that took over the entire known world. Why? People were around to say, "I know it seems unbelievable, but I was there. That's exactly what happened."

Another question people have is, "Why so many translations?" Actually, the answer to that one is easy. The Bible was basically written in two languages: Hebrew and Greek. The Old Testament was written in the language of its writers—Hebrew—and the New Testament was written in the most-used language of its day—Greek. That means all of our Bibles today are translations of those original languages. This is why scholars who do such translating study Hebrew and Greek. Translations are necessary for every ancient manuscript, whether it's the writings of Plato or the writings of Virgil. It's true for more recent writings that weren't written in, say, English. If you read Dostoevsky's *The Brothers Karamazov* in English, you're reading a translation from the original Russian. Whatever language it was originally written in—Greek, Hebrew, Latin, French, Russian, or German—if it wasn't originally written in English and you read it in English, it's a translation. So when people ask, "How can you believe the Bible with so many translations?," this is a misunderstanding of what a translation is, as all ancient manuscripts are translated.

But why are there so many *different* translations? Again, that's easy too. It's not because we don't know what the original Hebrew and Greek manuscripts contain. It's because language changes so much. *Gay* used to mean being happy; now it means having a same-sex orientation. *Wicked* used to be something bad; now it means something is good—as in saying something is "wicked good." *Spam* used to be canned meat. Or something like meat. Whatever it was/is, you ate it instead of deleting it from your email inbox. *Cool* used to mean "cold," *Coke* was a drink not a drug, if someone was *hot* they were on fire, and your *booty* was your treasure. Not your . . . booty. Just think how our online world has changed what we mean by a *troll, friend, stream, mention,* or *cloud*. This is why dictionaries are always being updated. They have to be.

So when the Bible was translated in the 1600s, the Greek and Hebrew manuscripts were translated into the language of that day. That meant that there were lots of *thees* and *thous* and *heretofores* and other words we don't use today, or that don't even make sense. That's why the King James Bible is called the *King James* Bible: the translation was commissioned by King James and employed what is commonly called "King James English." But there's nothing magical or holy about King James English and we don't talk in King James English today. This is why more modern translations from the original Hebrew and Greek manuscripts are continually being produced for ease of reading and understanding in light of the ever-evolving makeup of modern language.

The Bible Is Inspired

Which brings us to our fourth and final headline. For those of us who are Christians, this isn't a normal book. It's inspired by God and we shouldn't water that word down. Sometimes we use the word *inspired* to mean that something was wonderfully creative, such as a painting by Rembrandt, or music by Bach, or a play by Shakespeare. Sometimes we use the word to refer to something that we feel—how we find a beautiful sunset or a powerful speech inspiring. Inspiration, as it relates to the Bible, is much more profound. When the apostle Paul was describing it in his second letter to Timothy, he put it this way:

> But you must remain faithful to the things you have been taught. You know they are true, for you know you can trust those who taught you. You have been taught the holy Scriptures from childhood, and they have given you the wisdom to receive the salvation that comes by trusting in Christ Jesus. All Scripture is inspired by God and is useful to teach us what is true and to make us realize what is wrong in our lives. It corrects us when we are wrong and teaches us to do what is right. God uses it to prepare and equip his people to do every good work. (2 Tim. 3:14–17 NLT)

The Greek word Paul used for *inspired* literally meant "God-breathed." That's the idea behind the inspiration of the Scriptures. Breathed out by God, exhaled by God, produced by God.

It's not a human book. It was written by humans, but as they were moved by God. It reflects their personality, vocabulary, and writing style, but the act of writing itself was stirred by God. More than three thousand times in the Bible we find the writers using some form of the expression "The Lord says." The prophet Jeremiah recorded God saying to him, "I [God] have put my words in your mouth" (Jer. 1:9). The idea of inspiration is that God used people to write the books of the Bible but was so involved in the process that they wrote exactly what he wanted. One of the clearest expressions of this idea was given by the apostle Peter: "Above all, you must realize that no prophecy in Scripture ever came from the prophet's own understanding, or from human initiative. No, those prophets were moved by the Holy Spirit, and they spoke from God" (2 Pet. 1:20–21 NLT).

About Interpretation

Now let's talk about how to interpret what you read. Because isn't that where it gets sticky? At least, that's what you hear, right? Every time somebody points out something the Bible says, somebody else will say, "Well, that's just your interpretation," as if when it comes to what the Bible says, there's nothing more than personal opinion. But is that true? Is interpreting the Bible just the reader's opinion, completely subjective, so that when it comes to the Bible, it's a free-for-all? You know . . . believe what you want, read it how you wish, because it doesn't say anything definitive. I'm afraid that's a cultural myth. There's an actual field of study for interpretation called *hermeneutics*, defined as "the science of interpretation." And it is a science—a series of steps, practices, disciplines, and rules that apply to interpretation.

But make no mistake—99 percent of the Bible doesn't take any heavy lifting in regard to interpretation. Here's some quick reading. In the Old Testament book of Deuteronomy, it says, "Hear, O Israel: The LORD our God, the LORD is one" (Deut. 6:4). So is there one God or two? One! In the Old Testament book of Exodus, it says, "You shall not steal" (Exod. 20:15). Is it okay to steal or not? It's not! In the New Testament book of 1 Thessalonians, it says, "Jesus died and rose again" (1 Thess. 4:14). Did Jesus die and rise again or not? The Bible says that he did. So is the Bible obscure in meaning? No. So why do so many claim that the Bible is difficult to understand? For some, it's not in trying to grasp the most obvious reading, but in accepting the *implications* of that reading. It's interesting how when you don't like something you read, you can suddenly find yourself believing it's hard to understand.

Lee Strobel says to pretend that your daughter and her boyfriend are going out for a Coke on a school night. You say to her, "You must be home before 11:00." Now suppose it gets to be 10:45 and the two of them are still having a great time. They don't want the evening to end, so suddenly they begin to have difficulty interpreting your instructions. They say: "What did he really mean when he said, '*You* must be home before 11:00'? Did he literally mean us or was he talking about *you* in a general sense, like people in general? Was he saying, in effect, 'As a general rule, people must be home before 11:00'? Or was he just making the observation that generally, people are in their homes before 11:00? I mean, he wasn't very clear, was he?

"And what did he mean by, 'You *must* be home before 11:00'? Would a loving father be so adamant and inflexible? He probably meant it as a suggestion. I know he loves me, so isn't it implicit that he wants me to have a good time? And if I am having fun, then he wouldn't want me to end the evening so soon.

"And what did he mean by, 'You must be *home* before 11:00'? He didn't specify *whose* home. It could be anybody's home. Maybe he meant it figuratively. Remember the old saying 'Home is where the heart is'? My heart is right here, out having a Coke, so doesn't that mean I'm already home?

"And what did he really mean when he said, 'You must be home before *11:00*'? Did he mean that in an exact, literal sense? Besides, he never specified 11:00 p.m. or 11:00 a.m. And he wasn't really clear on whether he was talking about Central Standard Time or Eastern Standard Time. I mean, it's still only quarter to seven in Honolulu. And as a matter of fact, when you think about it, it's *always* before 11:00. Whatever time it is, it's always before the next 11:00. So with all of these ambiguities, we can't really be sure what he meant at all. If he can't make himself more clear, we certainly can't be held responsible."[2]

There's no doubt that some parts of the Bible are hard to understand. It reflects the places, histories, cultures, and languages of places long ago and far away. Sometimes it helps to have some background information on those issues to get the best sense of it, and there are some passages that people might disagree about. But on the essential teachings and issues, the Bible leaves little room for confusion. As Mark Twain was known to have quipped, "It's not the parts of the Bible I don't understand that disturb me, rather it's the parts of the Bible that I *do* understand that disturb me."

But while truth can be disturbing, it is always life changing. The Bible gives guidance for virtually every area of life—work, marriage, family, relationships, finances, emotions, physical health—and millions, right now, today, are finding that it is guidance that *works*. People who have studied the Bible and faithfully applied its wisdom to their life say that it has transformed their lives. They will tell you that it has saved their marriage, helped them straighten out their finances, repaired broken relationships, and revolutionized their attitude toward work. Most importantly, they will tell you that it has shown them how to be in an ever-deepening and vibrant relationship with the living God.

Okay, so much for what Christians say the Bible is; what you are probably ready to ask and explore is whether the Bible, as a writing, examined critically, is credible.

It's a fair question.

The Bible's Textual Credibility

The Bible is an old book that has been copied thousands of times over a period of centuries. So is the text we have even reliable? Can we know what the authors of the Bible really wrote after all of this time? The integrity of any ancient writing is determined by the number of documented manuscripts or fragments of manuscripts we have to examine. For example, there are only nine or ten good manuscripts of Julius Caesar's *Gallic Wars* in existence, the oldest of which is a copy dating about nine hundred years *after* his time. Yet no historian that I am aware of has serious doubts about the reality of Caesar, or of the integrity of the text itself. There are also fewer than ten existing copies of the ancient manuscripts of Plato that are available to study and compare in order to determine the accuracy and quality of the transmission of his writings throughout the years. The oldest of these manuscripts is a copy dating about *fourteen hundred years* after it was originally written. Still, you do not have scholars discounting the historicity of the writings of Plato, or expressing concern that what we have of Plato's writings is less than true to his original thoughts.[3]

When it comes to the Bible, there are more than *five thousand* handwritten manuscripts in the Greek language in support of the New Testament *alone* that help us ensure the accuracy of

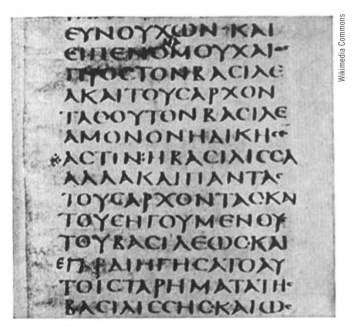

Wikimedia Commons

A fragment of the Codex Sinaiticus containing the Greek version of Esther 1:16–17 its writings. Many of the earliest copies are separated from the originals not by fourteen hundred years, nor even nine hundred years, but by only twenty-five to fifty years.[4] The Old Testament is equally rich, supported by such findings as the famous Dead Sea Scrolls in 1947, providing manuscripts a thousand years older than any previously known Hebrew manuscripts of the Bible and representing almost every book of the Old Testament.[5] Without a doubt, the Bible is the most documented ancient writing in all of history in terms of textual credibility.[6]

The Bible's Historical Credibility

But simply because a text may be sound doesn't mean that what it records is historically *accurate*. When the Bible *says* that something happened, did it *really* happen? The text may have been preserved with integrity, but that doesn't mean that what it says is *true*. As a result, the historical credibility of the Bible demands investigation.

Interestingly, many of the writers of the Bible invite such examination by claiming to be eyewitnesses to what they wrote, or to have conducted such research themselves! For example, one of the four biographers of Jesus, a physician named Luke, writes the following at the start of his account:

> Many have undertaken to draw up an account of the things that have been fulfilled among us, just as they were handed down to us by those who from the first were eyewitnesses and servants of the word. With this in mind, since I myself have carefully investigated everything from the beginning, I too decided to write an orderly account for you . . . so that you may know the certainty of the things you have been taught. (Luke 1:1–4)

And the apostle John wrote this in one of his contributions to the New Testament:

That which was from the beginning, which we have heard, which we have seen with our eyes, which we have looked at and our hands have touched—this we proclaim. (1 John 1:1)

But merely claiming to convey factual historical truth as eyewitnesses has little to do with whether the actual writings are true. How has the Bible stood up under outside examination? Of particular interest to many is, understandably, archaeological evidence. Sir William Ramsay of Oxford University, regarded as one of the greatest archaeologists ever to have lived, concluded upon his own examination that the writers of the Bible are historians of the first rank who should be placed along with the very greatest of historians. So overwhelming was the support of the archaeological evidence that Ramsay eventually became a Christian.[7] Dr. W. F. Albright, late professor emeritus of Johns Hopkins University, declared that there can be no doubt that archaeology has confirmed the historicity of the Bible.[8] Historian and archaeologist Joseph P. Free notes that recent discoveries have "produced material that confirm the Scriptures at point after point."[9]

For example, the book of Genesis makes mention of the infamous cities of Sodom and Gomorrah, which were destroyed for their utter abandonment to wickedness. No record of such places existed outside of the biblical record, leading many to question the Bible's historical credibility. Now, archaeologists have unearthed the place of pagan worship for the inhabitants of the two cities at Bab edh-Dhra, including evidence of sudden and unexplainable destruction in approximately 2,000 BC. The remains of the place were covered in layers of ash and sulfur, which, as the Bible records, is how the cities were destroyed when fire was rained down on them in judgment.[10] Furthermore, scientists discovered that a "superheated blast from the skies"—possibly a meteor—decimated cities found near the Dead Sea 3,700 years ago. Biblical analysts feel this clearly echoes the destruction of Sodom.[11]

Wikimedia Commons

Sodom and Gomorrah ruins uncovered at Bab edh-Dhra

Even entire civilizations, such as the Hittites, were unknown outside of the Bible. Since a review of the known literature of the day revealed no mention of such people, the conclusion was that the Bible was simply in error. Then, the capital city of the Hittite empire was discovered, as well as forty other cities that made up the empire.[12] Another example is King David. He is mentioned more than a thousand times in the Bible yet, until recently, no record of such a person could be found outside of the Bible. This led some to put the biblical King David on the same footing as the mythical King Arthur. Then, in 1993 and 1994, at the northern Israelite site of Tel Dan, pieces of a three-thousand-year-old monumental basalt stone were found that bore inscriptions about the "King of the House of David."[13] It was the first non-Biblical attestation of David's existence.

Even something as seemingly minor as a biblical mention of Jesus and his disciples being out on a boat on the Sea of Galilee has raised questions. No boats of that nature had ever been

The stone found in Tel Dan bearing the description of the "King of the House of David"

found, much less ones that would have carried Jesus and all twelve of his disciples, as the New Testament claims. Then, during a severe drought in the mid-1980s that brought the Sea of Galilee to unusually low levels, two brothers discovered the remains of a two-thousand-year-old boat buried in the mud along the shore. Dating to the very time of Christ, the boat could either be rowed or sailed and could hold up to fifteen men, perfectly matching the New Testament descriptions.

Recently, in Jerusalem's "City of David" dig site, archaeologists unearthed a 2,600-year-old stone with the names of people found in the Bible—specifically Nathan-Melech, who is mentioned in the second book of Kings as an official to King Josiah (see 2 Kings 23:11)—discovered among the ruins of a building destroyed by the Babylonians. Doron Spielman, vice president of the City of David Foundation, said of these findings: "The ongoing archeological excavations at the City of David continue to prove that ancient

Wikimedia Commons

The boat found in the Sea of Galilee dating back to the time of Christ

Jerusalem is no longer just a matter of faith, but also a matter of fact. It is truly fascinating to watch how archeologists have uncovered more than twelve layers of Jerusalem history in what used to be a parking lot until just few years ago."[14]

There are so many more archaeological finds we could talk about. We've found the burial box of Caiaphas—the high priest Jesus was brought to for his trial before his crucifixion. We've found inscriptions related to Pontius Pilate, the fifth governor of Roman Judea, also a key player in the trial and crucifixion of Jesus. Advanced photographic techniques also revealed an inscription on a seal ring stating "of Pilates" and would likely have been worn by someone who was able to act on Pilate's authority.[15] We've found inscription support for the Philistine empire, prominently featured in the Old Testament, giving support to the very names of the leaders and cities that the Bible records. Even the signature seal of the prophet Isaiah has been discovered.[16]

But here's the real headline: not only have the Bible's claims been *supported* through archaeological research, there has *never* been an archaeological discovery that has ever *refuted* a single biblical claim. Renowned Jewish archaeological expert Dr. Nelson Glueck has observed, "It may be stated categorically that no archaeological discovery has ever controverted a biblical reference."[17] In fact, there have been so many archaeological discoveries that

The signature seal of the prophet Isaiah found at the foot of the southern wall of Jerusalem's Temple Mount

have supported the Bible that Dr. John Warwick Montgomery, then dean of the Greenleaf Law School, noted that if you were to apply the Federal Rules of Evidence to the Gospel records, "this rule would establish competency in any court of law."[18]

The Bible's Authoritative Credibility

Which leads to the question of the Bible's *authoritative* credibility as a spiritual text. Ultimately, the real question is whether this text is truly from God. We've already explored how this rises and falls on where you stand with Jesus. But what if that's unsettled for you? Is there anything else to consider? One area that many have explored relates to prophecy. I know, the very idea of a "prophet" or "prophecy" seems planted in the realm of myth. But let's play it out. If the supposedly "inspired" authors of the Bible foretold events with accuracy, and were *never wrong* in these prophecies, it would be convincing evidence of the Bible's authoritative credibility. If such prophecies did not come true, or were (at best) average in their success rate, the Bible's position as an authoritative text would be dramatically weakened.

How does the Bible fare by such an examination? Let's just consider the prophecies surrounding the life and ministry of the Messiah, which Christians believe were made in relation to the coming of Jesus. In the Old Testament, almost eight hundred years prior to the birth of Jesus, there were prophecies about the place of the Messiah's birth, his ancestry, how he would be born, how he would be betrayed for a specific amount of money, how he would be put to death, how his bones would remain unbroken, and how the soldiers would cast lots for his clothing. Sound familiar? If you know anything about the life and death of Jesus, they should, because *every one of them took place in his life.*[19]

Now, what would be the odds of each one of those prophecies being fulfilled in minute detail, having come about—through chance—in the life and person of Jesus? This must be asked, because a questioning mind can simply say that the biblical prophecies in relation to the life of Jesus are just coincidence. Scientist and mathematician Dr. Peter Stoner, former chair of the department of mathematics and astronomy at Pasadena City College and later chair of the department of science at Westmont College, worked on this with six hundred of his students. Their goal was to calculate the odds for the detailed accuracy of just *one* biblical prophecy about the coming Messiah to have come true in the life of Jesus the way it did. Eventually they determined that the odds of such an event were 1-in-400 million. Stoner and his students then calculated what the odds would be to have *eight* of the prophecies made about the Messiah be specifically fulfilled in Jesus *by chance.* The odds came out to be 1-in-10^{17}. That's a figure with seventeen zeros behind it!

$$100,000,000,000,000,000$$

Stoner then went on to look at the odds of forty-eight prophecies about the Messiah being fulfilled, by chance, in the life and person of Jesus. His conclusion is that it would be 1-in-10[157] for all of them to have come true in the life of just one person in history.[20] Yet this is precisely what happened. Not with merely forty-eight prophecies, but with up to 332 distinct Old Testament prophecies concerning the Messiah that were fulfilled in the life of Jesus.[21] For this to have happened by chance would be akin to a person randomly finding a predetermined atom among all the atoms in a trillion, trillion, trillion, trillion, billion universes the size of our universe.[22] For anyone who is trying to determine whether or not to give authoritative credibility to the Bible, the odds are overwhelming—based on prophecy *alone*—that the Bible is the inspired Word of God.

The Bible's Internal Credibility

So, the Bible stands up textually, it stands up historically in terms of outside evidence, but now let's consider another area: *contradictions*. Because isn't that what you hear so many people say about the Bible? That it contradicts itself? Let's begin with what a contradiction is. In any introductory course on philosophy, you learn about the law of noncontradiction or logical fallacy. In essence, it means that A and non-A cannot both be true. That would be a contradiction. You can't say "It's raining" and "It's not raining" and have both be true. You can't say "It's hot" and "It's cold" and have both be true. That is the nature of a contradiction.

So a biblical contradiction would be like Mark's biography of Jesus in the Bible saying Jesus died on the cross, and then Luke's account saying Jesus didn't die or that he died falling off a donkey. But if you have Mark's biography record something that Jesus said on the cross, and John's account includes *something else* Jesus said—or even leaves out some of what Mark recorded—that's not a contradiction. John's account does not contradict what Mark recorded—John just included another detail. Or, John didn't include a detail that Mark did.

So consider a common citation of a supposed contradiction in the Bible. In Mark's account of the death of Jesus, there is an emphasis on Jesus's agony. In Luke's account, there is a focus on Jesus's concern for His mother. But that's not a contradiction. He could have been in agony *and* concerned for his mother! Here's another one to consider. In Matthew's account, we are told that Peter will deny Jesus before the cock crows, and in Mark's account we are told that Peter will deny Jesus before the cock crows twice. Again, that's not a contradiction. Peter would deny Jesus before the cock crowed, but Mark simply supplies an added detail— that the cock wouldn't just crow once, but twice. Not exactly a scandal. Which is why whenever someone tries to tell me that the Bible contradicts itself, I ask them, "Do you *know* that to be true, or are you just buying into an urban legend?" Then I simply ask them to show me one.

But there is one "contradiction" that does seem robust, and it's the seeming conflict between the God of the Old Testament and the God of the New Testament. The Old Testament is a record of God's covenants or agreements with people before the time of Christ. As time went on, the covenants gave more and more of God's plan, more and more of God's revelation, building toward the supreme revelation of God's plan, which the Old Testament said would be the coming of the Messiah—God himself—to save the world.

Which brings us to the New Testament.

The New Testament is the new agreement God made with men and women about how to be in a relationship with God after the coming of Christ. It didn't replace the old covenants—it fulfilled them. God's agreements with people and the nation of Israel in the Old Testament contained signs of what was to come, and these all found their fulfillment in the new covenants established through Jesus. All along, God's intention was to bring forth the Savior of the world in the person of Jesus. The very purpose of the old covenant, or what is often called the law, was to prepare the people for the coming, complete covenant that would arrive with the Messiah.

Once Jesus came and we received the New Testament, did that mean that we could just throw the Old Testament out? No. It still stands. But it needs to be read in light of its fulfillment in the New Testament. So does the law of the Old Testament apply to us at all today? Yes! The law provides us with a paradigm of time-less ethical, moral, and theological principles. But some laws no longer have validity because they have been completely fulfilled in Christ.

Take the famous "eye for an eye" idea. In the Old Testament, it says this:

> The punishment must match the injury: a life for a life, an eye for an eye, a tooth for a tooth, a hand for a hand, a foot for a foot, a burn for a burn, a wound for a wound, a bruise for a bruise. (Exod. 21:23–25 NLT)

But in the New Testament, Jesus said this:

> You have heard the law that says the punishment must match the injury: "An eye for an eye, and a tooth for a tooth." But I say, do not resist an evil person! If someone slaps you on the right cheek, offer the other cheek also. (Matt. 5:38–39 NLT)

So which is it? Is it an "eye for an eye" as it says in the Old Testament or "turn the other cheek" as Jesus said in the New Testament? The answer is simple: "Yes!" The "eye for an eye" passage in Exodus 21 was all about whether you could pursue private vendettas and retaliate when you had been wronged. And the answer was "no." That was for the judges to decide. Instead, they were to follow a principle based on "an eye for an eye," meaning compensation and restitution in direct proportion to the crime. They were to match the damages inflicted and no more. You were not to have blood feuds or private wars. So "an eye for an eye" was a literary device to give a formula for compensation. But then Jesus gave its fulfillment in the New Testament, essentially saying, "You have heard of 'eye for eye'—and that's good—but I tell you to go further! Don't retaliate at all! Don't harbor a spirit of resentment. If someone does you wrong, meet it by doing them something right!"

That kind of fulfillment ran throughout Jesus's teaching. Over and over the *letter* of the law was met with the greater, more challenging *spirit* of the law. Jesus would say, "You have heard you are not to commit adultery—but I tell you, don't lust in your heart!" "You've heard not to commit murder—I tell you, don't hate!" (see Jesus's Sermon on the Mount found in Matt. 5). Jesus wanted to take the law and put it in people's hearts. So there's no contradiction—just bringing the law to its fullest expression and application.

The Bible and Science

Right about now, you might be thinking about things the Bible says that may not contradict itself, but that put it at odds against science. In other words, what do you do when science contradicts the Bible? For example, God creating the heavens and the earth in six days, making the universe less than ten thousand years old. We know that simply isn't true. So how is this reconciled? It's quite easy. The Bible doesn't teach that idea.

This is probably a good time to delve into the larger relationship between the Bible and science. The Bible does not pretend to position itself as a textbook on science. It doesn't even try to answer most of the questions that science is asking. This is extremely important to understand, because most of the supposed conflicts between science and the Bible come when people try to make the Bible speak outside of what it is intending to. Why? It's a Hebrew book.

There are three ways of looking at reality, at least in Western thinking. First, there is the Greek way, which is largely descriptive and explanatory. The Greek way of looking at the world has an emphasis on rationality. Aristotle, for example, felt that once you defined a thing, you had exhausted its essence. When you approach something with Greek questions, you tend to be searching for shape and substance and definition. So one might approach water and ask, "*What* is water?" "What does it *look* like?" "What does it *feel* like?" Description. That's the Greek way.

A second way of looking at reality can be termed the Latin way, which is primarily concerned with method. Latin questions ask: "How does this *work*?" "How do we *do* this?" "What are the *steps* involved?" Most of us tend to look at the world in Greek and Latin ways because we are the product of a Greek and Latin culture. So it's natural for us to take our Greek and Latin questions to the Bible. The problem is that you can't always ask Greek or Latin questions of the Bible, because it's not a Greek or Latin book! It's

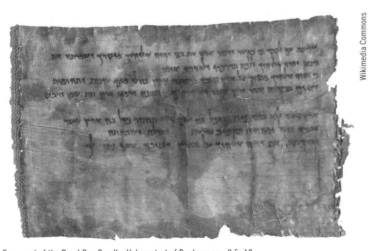

Wikimedia Commons

Fragment of the Dead Sea Scrolls, Hebrew text of Deuteronomy 8:5–10

Hebrew, which is an entirely different way of looking at reality. The Old Testament was written by Hebrews and in Hebrew. The New Testament may have been written in Greek, but it was with a Hebrew worldview. And the Hebrew way of looking at things was very different than the Greek or Latin way.

The Hebrew mind was concerned with what a thing was for and did it work. Matters of use, utility, and value were paramount. This is why you can read all four biographies of the life and teaching of Jesus and never once find a physical description of Jesus. Four biographies, four different authors, yet he's never described physically in any of them. To the Hebrew mind, it simply wasn't important. It probably never entered their mind to describe him. Or consider when we read that an angel visited someone in the Bible, the question was never, "What did he look like?" That wasn't important to a Hebrew. Their question was always, "What does he want us to do?"[23]

Now we can return to the Bible and science. When you read the book of Genesis you find that it says two main things about creation: God did it, and it was good. That's it. Now, if you are inclined toward a Greek or Latin sensibility, you want to know *how* God did it. But Genesis doesn't tell us how God did it, only *that* he did it. Why? It's a Hebrew book. I know what you're feeling: "But I want Greek and Latin answers to my Greek and Latin questions!"

Get used to disappointment.

But some people don't want to get used to disappointment. So they force the Bible to be something it's not, and force it to answer things it doesn't. And that's what has created the conflict people *think* exists between science and the Bible. For example, people read Genesis through a Greek or Latin lens, reading that God created the heavens and the earth in six days and rested on the seventh day, and they interpret this to be a succession of twenty-four-hour solar days. From that, they use the histories and genealogies in the Bible and calculate that—according to what they've read—the age of Earth is less than ten thousand years old. Meaning, therefore, that all of the scientific evidence we looked at earlier of the Big Bang happening about 13.8 billion years ago and Earth being 4.5 billion years old is just wrong. That light we see coming from stars billions of light-years away, the geological stratigraphy we see in places like the Grand Canyon ranging from 200 million to 2 billion years ago, and the age of the fossils of dinosaurs has to be either ignored or dismissed by spending incredible amounts of energy on scientifically dubious theories that try to explain it all away in light of a young Earth.

Yes, there are some people who read the Bible and interact with science this way. Not many, but some. I can't speak for them. I can speak for the vast majority of Christians who say that in no way, shape, or form does reading the Bible make you hold to that view.[24]

The mention of seven days was just an ancient, poetic way of talking about the fact that God did it. People who try to make it a scientific statement about seven literal, twenty-four-hour days simply aren't reading the text carefully. You may say, "But aren't Christians supposed to take the Bible literally?" Absolutely, but in this case, that's not taking it literally *enough*. To read the Bible literally means you read it the way it was intended to be read. Which means you take it the way it was written, in accordance with its genre, in light of its language and the time in which it was written. If you take Genesis 1 and 2 literally, as they were *actually* written, then you have to read them as poetic description because that's what they were. That was their genre. They weren't trying to be a scientific treatise. How could God have intended to inspire the writer to convey scientific precision about literal, twenty-four-hour solar days when, according to the text, the sun and the moon weren't even created until the fourth day! You couldn't have even *had* a twenty-four-hour solar day until the fourth day—because there was nothing in existence that was solar! I think God could have inspired the writer to be a little more careful on that one if he meant it to be a scientific statement.

The account also says that on the seventh day God rested. Since when does an omnipotent, omniscient Being need to take a day to rest? That's not only bad science, it's bad theology. Clearly, this is poetic, figurative language. And if that's not enough, the word used in the original Hebrew language for *day* is the word *yom* that, while it can be defined as a twenty-four-hour solar day, can also mean a segment of time—weeks, a year, several years, an age, or even an era. We use the word *day* in a similar way today, talking about our "grandfather's day" or about "days gone by." The use of the word *day* in Genesis could have stood for any period of time, even indefinite periods. It was a literary device, not a scientific declaration. The days in Genesis, if they carried any parallel to what happened scientifically, were indefinite periods of time allowing for everything from the dinosaurs to the Ice Age. The supposed tension between the Bible and science in regard to the age of Earth is really nonexistent. Nothing in the Bible would go to war against the universe being about 13.8 billion years old, and Earth about 4.5 billion years old, which are currently the best estimates of science.

Now you might be wondering about all the other stuff that seems to pit the Bible and science against each other, such as miracles. And it's true—the Bible is full of supernatural events, everything from the parting of oceans, to the feeding of thousands with a few loaves of bread and some fish; from the stopping of Earth's orbit, to the resurrection of the dead. Some would say, "Listen, you just can't have the disruption of the physical laws of the universe that way. Miracles are impossible." And they would be absolutely right. They are impossible. The Bible's record of miracles is guilty of flying in the face of what science would say can happen. But while a scientific dilemma, it is not a particularly large intellectual (much less spiritual) dilemma. Not if there is a God. If you admit to the possibility of a God, then miracles aren't an issue. Because a miracle, by its very definition, is the suspension of the physical laws of the universe. They are supernatural interventions that circumvent the natural laws. That's what makes them miraculous. MIT professor Ian Hutchinson, author of *Can a Scientist Believe in Miracles?*, suggests that miracles should not be seen as God intervening in the natural order of things. Because the regular order of things that we explore through science is completely dependent on God's will, a miracle is "an extraordinary act of God" by which God "upholds a part of the universe in a manner different from the normal."[25] So if there is a God on the loose, miracles are no big deal. As journalist Rebecca McLaughlin put it: "To believe in the God of the Bible who created the universe and not to believe in miracles is rather obtuse. It would be like my daughters believing their dad could make bread from scratch (which he can) but that he couldn't toast a Pop-Tart."[26] Miracles just mean there is something and more specifically Someone bigger than science.

So that's a bit about the Bible. But as much as Christians might be called a "people of the book," Jesus did not come simply to cement a set of authoritative writings as religious canon. He came to fulfill God's redemptive plan, to establish the new community—to write the final chapter on not simply another story, but *the* story.

And it is to that story we now turn.

6

THE CHURCH

I will put together my church, a church so expansive with energy
that not even the gates of hell will be able to keep it out.

Jesus (Matt. 16:18 Message)

I read of a pastor who boarded a plane in a pair of old blue jeans
and a polo shirt, looking anything but ministerial. He sat down
next to a well-dressed business guy who was reading a copy of
the *Wall Street Journal*. They exchanged the usual pleasantries,
and then the pastor asked the man what he did for a living. With
obvious pride, the man said: "Oh, I'm in the health and wholeness business. We can change anyone's self-concept by changing
their connection to themselves and their body. It's really a very
profound, powerful thing." He was a fairly young guy, so the pastor asked him if he had been doing it for very long.

"No," he said, "I just graduated from the University of Michigan's School of Business, but they've already given me so much
responsibility I hope to eventually manage the western part of
the operation."

"So you're a national organization?"

And he said, "Oh, yes. We are the fastest-growing company of our kind in the nation. It's really good to be a part of an organization like that, don't you think?" And the pastor nodded in approval. Then came the inevitable question.

"And what do you do?"

"It's interesting," the pastor said. "We actually have similar business interests. You're in the body-changing business, and I'm in the personality-changing business. In my field, we apply basic theocratic principles to accomplish indigenous personality modification." The guy had no idea what that meant, but he said, "You know, I've heard about that. Do you have an office here in the city?"

"Oh, yes. We have many offices, up and down the state," the pastor replied. "In fact, we're national; we have at least one office in every state of the union including Alaska and Hawaii." By this time, the young guy was racking his brain trying to identify this huge company that he must have heard about or read about somewhere.

The pastor went on: "Yep, in fact, we've gone international. And Management has a plan to put at least one office in every country of the world by the end of this business era." The pastor paused a minute and then asked, "Do you have that in your business?"

The guy said, "Well, no. Not yet. But you mentioned management. How do they make it work?"

"Actually," the pastor said, "it's a family business. There's a Father and a Son . . . they run everything."

The guy said, "Wow. That must take a lot of capital."

"You mean money? Yes, it does. No one knows just how much, but we never worry . . . Those of us in the Organization have a saying about our Boss, that 'He owns the cattle on a thousand hills.'"

"Oh," the guy said, "he's into ranching too? Wow. Well, what about you?"

"You mean the employees?" the pastor asked. "They are something to see. They have a 'Spirit' that pervades the organization. The Father and Son love each other so much that their love filters down so that we all find ourselves loving one another too. I know this sounds old-fashioned in a world like ours, but I know people in the organization who are willing to die for me. Do you have that in your business?"

"No," the man said, "not exactly. But what about your benefits? Are they good?"

"Good? They're amazing. I have complete life insurance, fire insurance—all the basics. You might not believe this, but it's true: I have holdings in a mansion that's being built for me right now for my retirement. Do you have that in your business?"

"Not yet," the young man said, by this time feeling like the health and wholeness market wasn't exactly the place to be. "But can your operation last? I mean, companies come and go."

The pastor said, "Oh, I think we've got a pretty good future. After all, we've got a two-thousand-year run going."[1]

Nothing compares to the church. No business, no investment, no enterprise, no activity. It's the heart of God's plan, and Christians believe it is the hope of the world. As such, it is our conviction that it's the most dynamic, active, vibrant, forceful project on the planet. It is the one thing we will give our lives to that will live on long after we are gone. And not just for a generation or two, but for all of eternity.

But that may not be what you have experienced.

I don't know what your background with church is, if you have any at all. Some grew up feeling church was boring and irrelevant, divided and nasty. Others dislike it because it epitomizes "organized religion," which is a euphemism for being lifeless, if not corrupt. All to say, many people, if they ever do get into the spiritual side of things, don't want church to be a part of the package. There's not a single thing about the church that captivates them—or, more to the point, that they think *should* captivate them.

So if all that's true, why have Christians made the church so central to their expression of the Christian faith? Because when the church is truly *being* the church, there is *nothing* more captivating.

Furthermore, Jesus made sure we know it's central to our expression of the Christian faith.

The Story

Let me tell you a story. And it's not just *a* story but *the* story. It's the story of all of human history. It's the story about what God is fundamentally about in this world. And what he is about is the church, the new community.[2]

To tell this story, we have to go all the way back to the very beginning. In fact, before the beginning. Because it begins with who God is. As we've already discussed, the Bible tells us that God is unique. He's triune: that is, three persons who are one God—God the Father, God the Son, and God the Holy Spirit. The idea of God being about community finds its essence and definition deep within the very being of God, for God himself is a community of three persons in one Being. God is love, and that love flows between the Father, Son, and Holy Spirit.

Now love, by its very nature, seeks to give of itself. And because God is himself a community of oneness, he created us to be a community of oneness as well. One with him and one with each other. Here's how it's described in the Bible:

> The LORD God said, "It is not good for the man to be alone. I will make a helper suitable for him." . . .
> The LORD God made a woman . . . and he brought her to the man. . . .
> That is why a man leaves his father and mother and is united to his wife, and they become one flesh.
> Adam and his wife were both naked, and they felt no shame. (Gen. 2:18, 22, 24–25)

When God created Adam, the Bible says that God was displeased with the fact that Adam was alone. Adam had vertical community with God, but no horizontal community with another human being, because he had no one else with whom he could be *together* in oneness. For there to be true oneness, there had to be a plurality of persons. The woman was created to "help" the man out of his aloneness so that together they could enter into the community of oneness that existed in the very nature of God and was being offered as a gift to humans upon their creation. That is why God decreed that they would become "one flesh." In God's math of community, one plus one equals one. And it truly was community. There is much in the line we read in the book of Genesis that says, "Now the man and his wife were both naked, but they felt no shame" (Gen. 2:25 NLT). This was more than moral innocence; it also symbolized the depth of relational transparency these two people had.

But then came what theologians have called "the fall." As long as the man and the woman were in a right relationship with God—the Creator of community—they were able to maintain their own oneness with each other. The moment they violated their relationship with God by turning their backs on him and going their own way, their oneness with God and with each other was shattered. And that is precisely what they did and what happened. Not only did sin separate humans from God, it separated them from each other. So what did Adam and Eve do after that happened? They clothed themselves, reflecting the first of many barriers that now came into being between humans, and then they hid themselves, reflecting the beginning of the relational divide between humans and God.

This was bigger than simply Adam and Eve. Their fall led to the ongoing disruption of community throughout the growing human race. Think of the fateful decision to build the infamous Tower of Babel that you have probably heard of. Later in Genesis, we read how the peoples of the earth came together to build a huge monument to themselves—naming themselves lord of all. There was no effort to come together in community under God

The Tower of Babel by Pieter Bruegel the Elder, 1563

according to God's design, but an effort to divorce themselves from community with God and create a distorted and perverted sense of oneness. But removed from the true oneness of God, the Author of community, their community was destroyed. God stepped in, in his mercy, and disrupted their efforts because he loved them too much to allow them to completely separate themselves from him and true community. They were then scattered all over the earth, and when they tried to communicate with each other, they found that they could not even understand each other's speech. In their attempt to build a false community based on false oneness, they lost the capacity to even communicate.

And that's how the first eleven chapters of Genesis end, bringing the primeval history of the world to a close. But in chapter 12, we see God's continued investment in the redemptive drama—God's continued effort to bring people into community with him and with each other. For in chapter 12, we find that God calls out a man named Abram, and through Abram, he begins the

Jewish people's relationship with God. God called them into a community—Israel—through which he reestablished the picture of his oneness, and their oneness with each other, to the entire world. God did not quit on us or on his plan to build community into his creation. Out of the wreckage of the old community, he drew together a new community. Abram was called to leave his old ways, his old home, his old community, and set out. God promised that he would make him into a great nation. God even changed his name from Abram, which means the father of one people, to Abraham, which means the father of many nations. Abraham accepted God's plan for the new community, a plan that would eventually seek to bring together—in one community—all the peoples of the earth.

The story of how this effort fared among the descendants of Abraham is a tale of unrelenting disasters, described at length in the Old Testament. Despite Abraham, God's covenant, the continued gift of godly leaders, judges, and prophets, the nation of Israel fell into repeated cycles of rebellion, apostasy, defeats, invasions, divisions, and exiles until, mercifully, God intervened again. And this intervention brought all of history to a defining moment—for that intervention was Jesus. Through Jesus, God's dream prevailed and the One who could and would save, came— the second Adam, the one who would fulfill oneness and offer that oneness to all of us.

When Jesus willingly died on the cross for our sins, it was for a reason. The vertical dimension of the cross suggests the restoration of our communion with God. It symbolizes the need and potential of every human being to enter into a saving relationship with God through Christ. It reestablishes that communion with him for which we were created but which was forfeited in the garden; we have continued this rejection individually with our own cumulative sinfulness. The horizontal dimension of the cross symbolizes the other aspect of community that the cross offers—that we can be reconciled not only to God, but to each other and be brought together to form one body. So, through Christ, there is the new community, in a new oneness with God and in a new oneness with each other. This is why Jesus boiled down the entire law of the Old Testament into two commandments: love God and love people. In his final prayer recorded in the Bible, in John 17, Jesus prayed for one thing: oneness among his followers. The language he used was fitting when he said, "I have given them the glory you gave me, so they may be one as we are one" (John 17:22 NLT). Jesus prayed for restoration of the oneness among humans entrusted to them in creation: a oneness made in the image of the oneness within the Trinity. For Jesus, the model of oneness among humans was nothing less than that found in the relationship between the Father and the Son and the Holy Spirit.

This leads us to the church, the new community. What began with Abraham and the people of Israel was brought into reality through the cross of Christ. The church is the new Israel. Following the resurrection of Jesus, the very birth of the church occurred on what is now called the day of Pentecost. On that day, the people heard and understood others speaking in various languages, declaring the wonders of God. It was the Tower of Babel in reverse. Due to the power of the Holy Spirit to mark God's true community of people, the many languages were made one. Harmony and unity were now possible through Christ. And the church reflects the oneness God intended in so many ways: relational unity; caring for others at their point of need, such as those who are poor and hungry and homeless; coming together as a body in their use of spiritual gifts; and, supremely, the extension of community to others through Christ. Because the heart of the church's mission is the invitation of others into community.

But even that isn't the final word. At the end of time, at the resurrection of all believers, God's people on earth will be transformed eternally into one body, a fully formed community. And heaven—the ultimate community, the glorified church united with Christ—will reign. So the church, the new community, is the centerpiece of history. The formation of that community of oneness is what history is all about. God has had one priority project throughout history, one that he will bring to climactic conclusion at the end of time—the formation of the new community. The church.

So no wonder we read these words from Jesus: "I [am putting] together my church, a church so expansive with energy that not even the gates of hell will be able to keep it out" (Matt. 16:18 Message). This is also why the earliest followers of Christ immediately joined in this new community and began forming and living the life of the church that was God's dream from the beginning. Here's how those early days were described in the New Testament:

> They devoted themselves to the apostles' teaching and to fellowship, to the breaking of bread and to prayer. Everyone was filled with awe at the many wonders and signs performed by the apostles. All the believers were together and had everything in common. They sold property and possessions to give to anyone who had need. Every day they continued to meet together in the temple courts. They broke bread in their homes and ate together with glad and sincere hearts, praising God and enjoying the favor of all the people. And the Lord added to their number daily those who were being saved. (Acts 2:42–47)

So the church is not some peripheral man-made organization. It is the centerpiece of history and the vanguard of God's mission. It's the very cause of Christ. And for the Christ follower? What it brings to bear on their life is irreplaceable. You can't be a fully devoted follower of Christ and live a life apart from his church, because Christ-following involves interacting with other Christ followers in the context of the church as Christ has designed it. In the Bible, we are told that Christ followers are to "serve one another" (Gal. 5:13), "encourage one another" (1 Thess. 5:11), "accept one another" (Rom. 15:7), "bear with . . . and forgive one another" (Col. 3:13). You can't do the "one anothers" without "another." Jesus went so far as to say that it would be the practice of community brought to life in and through the church that would offer the ultimate affirmation to the world about his own life and ministry. Here are his words:

> So now I am giving you a new commandment: Love each other. Just as I have loved you, you should love each other. Your love for one another will prove to the world that you are my disciples. (John 13:34 NLT)

And then, a few chapters later, it records his final prayer and it was for the same thing. He said,

> I am praying not only for these disciples but also for all who will ever believe in me through their message. I pray that they will all be one, just as you and I are one—as you are in me, Father, and I am in you. And may they be in us so that the world will believe you sent me. . . .
>
> May they experience such perfect unity that the world will know that you sent me and that you love them as much as you love me. (John 17:20–21, 23 NLT)

Jesus was absolutely convinced that it would be the church, functioning as the church, that would arrest the attention of the world and give ultimate affirmation to his message.

What / Where Is the Church?

So what is an authentic church community? I remember sitting in the boardroom of a prominent Christian business leader. They did a lot of "Christiany" things in this business. He told of the mission trips he had taken with his employees, the investments the company had made from its profits in select boutique ministry ventures, and the Bible study offered on campus for employees. I think I even remember the mention of a corporate chaplain.

Then, at the end, he said he wasn't personally involved in a local church because, after all, "We're the church too. This company is the church."

Inside I thought I was going to explode. Everything within me wanted to shout, "No, you are NOT! A company is *not* the body of Christ instituted as the hope of the world by Jesus himself, chronicled breathtakingly by Luke through the book of Acts, and shaped in thinking and practice by the apostle Paul through letter after letter now captured in the New Testament. A marketplace venture that offers itself on the New York Stock Exchange is not the entity that is so expansive with energy not even the gates of hell can withstand its onslaught. An assembly of employees in cubicles working for end-of-year stock options and bonuses is not the gathering of saints bristling with the power of spiritual gifts as they mobilize to provide justice for the oppressed, service to the widow and the orphan, and compassion for the poor."

So when *do* you have the church?

You have the church when you have the message of Christ being proclaimed. You have the church when you have true community being fleshed out—a community of Christ followers across generations and ethnicities, male and female, young and old. You have the church when there is the practice of the "one anothers"—loving, serving, bearing. You have the church when there is worship and service and spiritual growth, all coming together for the singular mission of seeing those far from God brought near to him. You have the church when the sacraments of the Lord's Supper (or communion) and baptism are being stewarded—times when something sacred is imparted to you. You have the church when there is the biblical structure of pastors providing leadership and oversight. And you have the church when you have the body of Christ operating as it was meant to, with all of the gifts coming together—leaders leading, administrators administrating, artists being artistic, and so on—and all of them coming together as one body.

When you have that, it's the most breathtakingly beautiful and powerful force on the planet.

Let me give you some pictures of this.

At a recent baptism service, a woman tweeted out a picture of her son being baptized. But it was what she tweeted along with it that stuck with me. She wrote how ten years ago I baptized her and her husband and now we baptized their son. To that she added the hashtags #liveschanged #familieschanged.

Another picture of this.

On a Thursday afternoon, a young woman came by one of our campus offices to give me something. I was in a meeting, so she left it at the front desk. On the back of the envelope I read, "I thought I was going to put this in an offering plate but I think it would be best to give to you directly." Here's what her letter said:

> I have been coming to your church. . . . I am 23. . . . When I was 12 years old I started cutting myself. Now my arms are covered in an overwhelming amount of scars, but I am proud to say there are no open cuts. I have not cut for probably a year now, but I still have razor blades that are hidden around my room. . . . I quit when I was about to cut one day but heard Jesus in my ear saying, "I bled enough." He took my pain on the cross and I no longer needed to take it out on myself. But I realized by holding on to razor blades I am not fully letting go of the pain and addiction to cutting. I want to fully let it go now. . . . It says in the Bible, "Cast all your anxiety on Him for He cares for you." So I'm doing that today. This is an of-fering plate and I am offering to Jesus today more than any amount of money I could ever offer Him. These are all my razor blades that I have kept hidden around in different places of my reach just in case. I am handing it over to God and I trust you also with this as well. Thank you for all you and this church have done in my life.

And with the letter were the razor blades.

One more picture. For Christians the heart of our mission is to the least and the lost. The least meaning those who are poor,

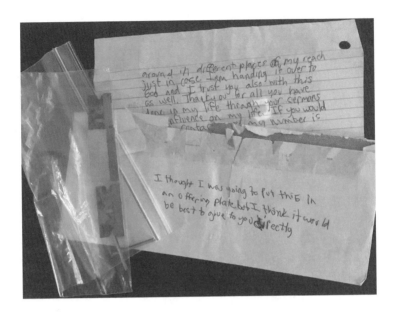

hungry, in need of shelter, oppressed, and abused. And the lost meaning those who are in need of God, in need of the saving message of Jesus, and in need of knowing how much he loves them and wants to wrap his arms around them. When it comes to the least and the lost, it's hard to imagine anyone in the world more abused, more in need of protection and rescue, more in need of hearing that God loves them more than they can imagine, than the children caught up in the sex trafficking industry throughout the world.

Some are runaways, some are kidnapped, some are sold into it by their fathers. But they are just children—eight or nine, maybe ten or twelve years old. They are taken, beaten, raped, and then plied with drugs or alcohol until they become addicts. That way, they can be controlled and forced to service up to twenty customers a day.

One of the worst places in the world for this is the Philippines. Our church found out that organizations such as the International

Justice Mission knew where these girls were, knew the dungeons below the brothels where they were kept, but couldn't rescue them until there was a place where they could go. They have no homes, and many can't return to their families because it was their fathers who sold them. They have addictions, psychological damage, need to be protected from their pimps while charges are brought, and need to be educated through all this. If you rescue and then just release, you are signing their death warrant. So, as horrific as it sounds, the girls are left in the brothels until there is not only a place to rescue them *from*, but to rescue them *to*. When we heard that, we said, "You just need a house? You're just talking bricks and mortar? We'll do that." So we built that house. We helped staff it. And once we did, they started rescuing children.

All to say, when the church is being the church, it really is the hope of the world. And not even the gates of hell can stand up under its onslaught.

So Why So Many Denominations?

So why are there so many denominations? Doesn't that undercut everything you've said about the power and beauty and centrality of the church? Good question. First, let's lay out what a "denomination" even is. The word itself comes from a Latin word that means "to name." So if you denominate something, you name it. You set it apart. You give it an identity, and that's what a religious denomination signifies. The *Dictionary of Christianity in America* puts it this way: "A Christian denomination is an association or fellowship of organizations within a religion that have the same beliefs or creed, engage in similar practices and cooperate with each other to develop and maintain shared enterprises."[3]

So how did so many get started?

Well, in truth, they've always been around. And what I mean by that is you have always had a diversity within the unity of

Christianity. Even in the earliest days of the burgeoning Christian movement. The various churches that sprung to life as Christianity exploded onto the scene were very different from each other. Not in terms of major doctrine, but in terms of style and culture and composition. So you had the high church in Rome that was a bit more formal, the church at Ephesus with the heavy emphasis on teaching, the charismatic church in Corinth, the predominantly black church that was probably started by the Ethiopian eunuch, and on it went. Different churches, different styles, yet all one in Christ and all birthed by the movement of the Holy Spirit, who seemed perfectly happy with the diversity. This helps explain one of the reasons why there are so many denominations. There are lots of different churches because there are a lot of different people, ethnicities, cultures, and stylistic preferences. In fact, Christianity has thousands of denominations around the world. Personally, I like the variety. I'm not wired like you, nor you like me. If you like "smells and bells" and I like drums and power chords—or both—that's okay.

But that's not the only reason why there are so many. A lot of the denominations started as protest groups against state-run religions. Throughout history, there have been established state or national churches. They still exist in many countries, particularly in Europe, such as the Church of England. So what did you do if you had a problem with a politically established religion? You had no choice but to start some kind of splinter group.

In America, several of the colonies tried to have an established church, but they didn't have enough of a majority to pull it off. So the various denominations became the norm, instead of just breakaway options from a state or national church. Throw in what came after the Revolution in terms of religious liberty and the separation of church and state, and then the rush of immigration that brought in all kinds of cultures and ethnicities, and you have what historian Sydney Mead has called "The Lively Experiment." This was America letting Christianity and individual Christians run free without state control. You want to start a church, you can start a church. You want to start a new denomination, have at it. And people did!

So has it been a good thing or a bad thing? Both. What's bad about it is that it gives the impression Christians can't get along with each other and that we fight and divide over stupid, petty things. Which, sadly, can be the case. Comedian Emo Philips wrote the following joke:

> Once I saw this guy on a bridge about to jump. I said, "Don't do it!" He said, "Nobody loves me." I said, "God loves you. Do you believe in God?"
>
> He said, "Yes." I said, "Are you a Christian or a Jew?" He said, "A Christian." I said, "Me, too! Protestant or Catholic?" He said, "Protestant." I said, "Me, too! What franchise?" He said, "Baptist." I said, "Me, too! Northern Baptist or Southern Baptist?" He said, "Northern Baptist." I said, "Me, too! Northern Conservative Baptist or Northern Liberal Baptist?"
>
> He said, "Northern Conservative Baptist." I said, "Me, too! Northern Conservative Baptist Great Lakes Region, or Northern Conservative Baptist Eastern Region?" He said, "Northern Conservative Baptist Great Lakes Region." I said, "Me, too! Northern Conservative Baptist Great Lakes Region Council of 1879, or Northern Conservative Baptist Great Lakes Region Council of 1912."
>
> He said, "Northern Conservative Baptist Great Lakes Region Council of 1912." I said, "Die, heretic!" And I pushed him over.[4]

It's fine to have different churches and denominations to reflect differences in personality and style and culture, but it's not fine if it reflects relational breakdowns. We are to be unified. Now, when the Bible talks about unity, it doesn't mean uniformity, which is everyone looking and thinking alike. And it doesn't mean unanimity, which is complete agreement about every little thing across the board. By unity, the Bible means first and foremost a oneness of heart—a *relational* unity. Being kind to one another, gracious to one another, forgiving of one another. Not assuming the worst, shooting the wounded, or being quick to be suspicious. Biblical unity is about working through conflicts, avoiding slander and gossip, and being generous in spirit. That's what Jesus was after. So when disunity in the worst sense is behind a denomination or splinter group, that's bad. But when it's just a "different strokes for different folks" kind of thing, it's not really that big of a deal. It's certainly no indictment of Christianity. It can actually be a positive thing. Most denominational divides are not hateful or mean spirited, or over big disagreements in the basic doctrines of the Christian faith. They are mostly about differences in preference. They reflect preferred styles of worship, patterns of organization, approaches to ministry, and understandings of custom and tradition. Think of it in terms of what people wear. Many of the differences among Christians are like the differences among people in the style of clothes that they wear. We are all humans underneath, but our clothes display our different personalities and cultures.[5] It would be a huge mistake to assume that the many churches and denominations within Christendom reflect a state of division and chaos. There is instead a unified set of beliefs that has been coupled with great freedom and diversity in the expression of that faith.

Protestant vs. Catholic

So what about the biggest divide within the Christian community—the divide between Protestants and Catholics? Same kind of situation? Mostly, but there is a bit more substance and history here. The earliest church, in the first forty or so years following the resurrection of Jesus, was essentially a movement within Judaism—a group who believed the Messiah had come in the person of Jesus. But then, around AD 70, Jerusalem fell to the Romans, and the

Christian movement was dispersed. The most important church that emerged, as you would imagine, was the one in Rome, which was the capital of the Roman Empire.

During the next few centuries, the church defined itself by four very important words: *one, holy, catholic,* and *apostolic.* First, the church was to be *one,* or unified. Second, it was to be a *holy* church, meaning set apart for God and separate from the world. Third, it was to be *catholic,* which simply meant "universal"; the church was to be a worldwide church, one that included all believers under its umbrella. So the word *catholic* was being used of the church long before any kind of institution within Christianity used it for its own name. Finally, the church was to be *apostolic,* meaning committed to the teaching handed down by Jesus through the apostles as contained in the New Testament.

A major turning point took place in Christian history in the year 312, when the Roman emperor Constantine converted to the Christian faith. This meant that the Christian church changed from being a persecuted minority to a faith that engulfed all of society, and Christendom was born. When the Roman Empire began to weaken, and the Early Middle Ages started—sometimes called

St. Peter's Square in Vatican City, Rome

Wikimedia Commons

the Dark Ages—the church was just about the only organization around to provide social glue. Particularly after the sacking of Rome by the Visigoths under the leadership of Alaric in AD 410. So the leaders of the church, known as popes, took center stage and gained enormous prestige and influence not just in the religious realm, but socially and politically.

As you might imagine, there were some divisions in the unity of the church. For example, in 1054 there was a split between the Western Latin church, which became the Roman Catholic Church, and the Eastern Greek church, which became known as the Orthodox Church. There were several issues related to the split, not the least of which was the Eastern Greek church's rejection of the supreme authority of the pope in Rome over the rest of the church. The term *pope*, which is Latin for *father*, was initially used for any bishop or church leader. Around the year 1100, it came to be used exclusively of the leader of the church at Rome, and with the split between East and West, he became the leader of the Western half of the church.

But that was nothing compared to the biggest historical division of all—one that would come in the sixteenth century and become known as the Protestant Reformation. There was a clear sense among several Catholic scholars, leaders, and intellectuals that the church had drifted away from the clear teaching of Scripture on some key issues, and it needed to be brought back in line with what the Bible taught. It is important to realize that the spirit of the Reformers was just that: reform. They never wanted to leave the Catholic Church, because that was the only manifestation of the church around. And they certainly never lost their understanding of the importance of the church. In fact, one of the leading Reformers, John Calvin, agreed with what Cyprian of Carthage said more than one thousand years earlier: "You cannot have God as your father unless you have the church for your mother." And he also agreed with Cyprian's other famous statement that, "Outside the church there is no hope of remission of sins nor any salvation."

Meaning, the church is the custodian of the gospel. It is the carrier and the communicator of Jesus's message.

The Reformers also agreed that the church should be one, holy, catholic, and apostolic, but they felt that the way those ideas had evolved under the medieval church's leadership was wrong. Which is why they were called "Protestants"—they were people in protest. Led by such men as Martin Luther, who posted his Ninety-Five Theses on the door of All Saints' Church in Wittenberg, Germany, in 1517, the Reformers began their great quest to restore the mother church to her biblical form.

Their effort failed.

In 1520, Luther himself was excommunicated by the pope and condemned by the Holy Roman Emperor. As a result, many, many Christians left what had been the mainstream church of the medieval era, forming the Lutheran and Reformed churches and, later, many other Protestant denominations including the Episcopal, Methodist, and Baptist churches. From that point on, the idea of there being "one" church could not be understood in either sociological or institutional terms, but only in theological terms. Arguably, this is what Jesus had in mind all along anyway. Yes, there are some theological differences. Most surround the role of the authority of Scripture in relation to the role of bishops and the pope, as well as the interplay between grace and faith when it comes to salvation. Yet both Protestants and Catholics believe that it is Jesus alone who saves. And we sign off together on the most ancient of Christian creeds, hammered out by the early Christian church in an effort to distill Christian orthodoxy, such as the Nicene Creed and the Apostles' Creed. So while Protestants believe that the Reformation was necessary, and that the one true church is no longer the one headquartered in Rome, there is still mutual respect and appreciation. And, even further, mutual enrichment. Most importantly, though, we all continue to stand under one very large umbrella—the umbrella of "mere Christianity."

Mere Christianity

The phrase "mere Christianity" was first used by the seventeenth-century Anglican writer Richard Baxter. Baxter lived through the English Civil War between the Protestants and the Catholics and, as a Protestant Puritan, Baxter threw his support behind Oliver Cromwell and the Parliamentary forces. Cromwell then summoned Baxter from his church in Kidderminster, Worcestershire, to help establish the "fundamentals of religion" for the new Protestant government. Baxter did what he asked, but Cromwell complained that Baxter's summary of Christianity could be affirmed by a Catholic. To which Baxter said, "Good!" Baxter refused to allow Christianity to divide people that way. Or to fall prey to the latest fashion or sect. Christianity was bigger than that. He was convinced that there was a core of orthodox Christianity that Puritans, Anglicans, and Catholics all affirmed and that should have been a source of peace among them.

Here's what he wrote in 1680:

> Must you know what Sect or Party I am of? I am against all Sects and dividing Parties: but if any will call Mere Christian by the name of a Party . . . I am of that Party which is so against Parties. . . . I am a CHRISTIAN, a MERE CHRISTIAN, of no other religion.[6]

Yes.

And it remains the hope of the world.

But let's be honest, that hope can sometimes be hard to hold when you interact with those who fill its ranks. So let's talk about that next.

7

UNCHRISTIANS

I like your Christ, I do not like your Christians. Your Christians are so unlike your Christ.

Gandhi[1]

Let's state the obvious. There are many "unchristian" Christians, specifically ones who are legalistic, judgmental, hypocritical, intolerant, and sexist. Aren't those the "big five"? And disliking these things in professing Christians makes it hard to get to the Christ they say they follow. So let's talk about it, beginning with legalism.

Legalism

Legalism is giving people a bunch of dos and don'ts to follow—in the name of God—that God did not say they needed to follow. It's a religion of added rules and regulations, standards and stipulations, codes and conduct, contrived by someone to determine who is, and who is not, spiritual. It's being asked—if not forced—to measure up in a way that can be binding and brutal, discouraging and defeating. And it feels about a million miles away from anything authentic, anything life changing, anything freeing.

Chuck Swindoll writes about a missionary family who had been sent to a place that did not have peanut butter. They happened to like peanut butter, and had young kids, so they arranged for some friends to send them a jar every now and then. Other missionaries in the area liked peanut butter, too, but since it wasn't available, they began to see being peanut butter free as a badge of spiritual honor. Almost defining what it meant to *be* spiritual. So much so, that when the new missionary family had it shipped in, others began to view them as somehow not quite sacrificing for Jesus. It got so bad, they ended up having to leave the mission field. The legalism was so petty, so unbelievably small-minded, the pressure so intense, that they returned to the States.

This is the nature of legalism. It reduces spirituality to outward practices and norms. I once read an article in the *Wall Street Journal* on UPS and how much pride they take in the productivity of their workforce. On average, a UPS driver delivers four hundred packages every working day. Here's how they do it: the corporation micromanages every detail of that driver's routine, using three thousand industrial engineers to dictate every single task. They are taught to step from their trucks with their right foot. They have to fold their money face-up. They have to carry their packages under their left arm. UPS tells their drivers how fast to walk from the truck to the point of delivery (it has to be three feet per second). They even tell them how to hold their keys, with the teeth up using their third finger. And if a driver is considered slow, they are accompanied on their route by a supervisor who pushes them through the steps with a clipboard and stopwatch. Now, for the package delivery business, it works. In the spirituality business, it doesn't and was never meant to.[2] Spirituality is not about religion or rituals, routines or rites . . . but relationship.

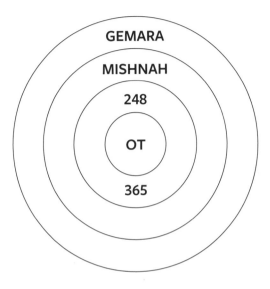

This is actually what caused the tension between Jesus and the religious leaders of his day—the "teachers of the law" and the group known as the Pharisees. They were very religious and were considered to be the holiest people of the day. They took the Old Testament and calculated that it contained 248 commandments and 365 prohibitions, and they lifted those commandments and prohibitions out and vowed to obey every single one. To make sure that they didn't break one of those rules, they made rules *about* the rules they made and laws *about* the laws! In the end, they came up with more than 1,500 additions. All of this oral tradition was later gathered into what is now known as the Mishnah. But even that wasn't enough, so they made more rules around the rules they had made in order not to break the rules they had made about the Scriptures. This created another circle they called the Gemara. Together, the Mishnah and the Gemara became known as the Talmud.

So how did rules about rules about rules play out for people like the Pharisees? To avoid taking the Lord's name in vain, they

CHRISTIANITY FOR PEOPLE WHO AREN'T CHRISTIANS

refused to even say God's name, even in honor and respect, worship and prayer. To avoid committing adultery, they would lower their heads whenever they passed a woman so that they wouldn't even look at her, because if they looked they might lust. This is why the most holy of all were known as "bleeding Pharisees" because they were lowering their heads so much they were always running into walls.[3] To properly follow the command to rest on the Sabbath and not work, they decided they needed to figure out how many steps you could take on those days without it becoming labor. For whatever reason, they calculated that to take anything beyond fifty steps on the Sabbath was work and, therefore, violated the law. They also decided that on holy days, a person could eat but not cook, could bandage a wounded person but not apply medicine. And if you were a woman, you couldn't look in the mirror because you might see a gray hair, and if you see a gray hair, you might be tempted to pluck it out, and plucking out a gray hair was considered work, and you couldn't work on the Sabbath.[4]

What did Jesus say about this? It was very direct: "And you experts in the law, woe to you, because you load people down with burdens they can hardly carry" (Luke 11:46). There are a couple of things to notice in that denunciation. First, the word *woe*. This was a very special word, a prophet's word. When a prophet uttered a word from God that was positive, they began with the word *blessed*. That is why in the Sermon on the Mount, Jesus said things like blessed are the pure in heart, blessed are the peacemakers, blessed are the merciful, and so on. When judgment was being uttered, a prophet began with the word *woe*. So we know exactly how Jesus felt about legalism. He "woed" it. He gave it the ultimate prophetic condemnation. And what was it about legalism Jesus hated? Not only did it kill the heart and cripple people's spiritual life, but it made a mockery of it. Because if it's all about legalism, then you can play the law like a tax lawyer. Chasing loopholes and technicalities, focusing on the letter of the law but never its spirit.

And that's what Jesus was after. Following Jesus is not about what you do, but about who you are. So if you're tired of legalism, this does not mean you're turned off to Christianity, much less Jesus. You're turned off to its counterfeit, which is a good thing. Here's what Jesus said was the real thing:

Are you tired? Worn out? Burned out on religion? Come to me. Get away with me and you'll recover your life. I'll show you how to take a real rest. Walk with me and work with me—watch how I do it. Learn the unforced rhythms of grace. I won't lay anything heavy or ill-fitting on you. Keep company with me and you'll learn to live freely and lightly. (Matt. 11:28–30 Message)

Judgmentalism

David Kinnaman and Gabe Lyons conducted a study on people who had turned away from the Christian faith and the church. The number one reason given was due to encountering people who were judgmental. We all know the type—people who are prideful, act morally superior, and find fault with everybody else. Judgmental people lack compassion, understanding, and grace toward other people's screwups. The judgmental seem more interested in condemning people than helping people.

If you have encountered this spirit, you have every right to be repulsed by it. It's a terrible thing to experience. Even more tragic is to find it among those who claim to be followers of Jesus. We all have a desire to receive grace—that incredible commodity that sees us for who we really are, not just for our mistakes, failures, and flaws; that dispenser of forgiveness; that spirit that restores those who have fallen, so amazing that we sing songs about this "Amazing Grace"; that powerful force unleashed on this planet by Jesus himself. So it can be incredibly devastating to discover that sometimes the *last place* it's found is with Jesus's people. Why does this happen? It's simple. Some Jesus people are not being very "Jesusy." Because Jesus went out of his way to tell those who followed him, "Whatever you do, don't judge people!" And if you don't think he went out of his way to make this patently clear, here are his words from the Sermon on the Mount:

> Do not judge others, and you will not be judged. For you will be treated as you treat others. The standard you use in judging is the standard by which you will be judged.
>
> And why worry about a speck in your friend's eye when you have a log in your own? How can you think of saying to your friend, "Let me help you get rid of that speck in your eye," when you can't see past the log in your own eye? Hypocrite! First get rid of the log in your own eye; then you will see well enough to deal with the speck in your friend's eye. (Matt. 7:1–5 NLT)

Jesus said, "Do not judge." Period. That's God's job, not ours. Now, to be fair, sometimes when people say, "Don't judge me" it's code for "Don't you dare say that anything I do is wrong or bad in any way." That's not what being judgmental is about. *Real* judgmentalism is about the practice of personal condemnation. The judgmental person Jesus is talking about is someone who is a fault-finder, who is negative and destructive toward other people. And when you encounter judgmentalism, remember it's not reflective of Jesus or the life he calls us to live. The real spirit of Jesus is truth, to be sure, but coupled with grace. Christians are nothing but a colossal collection of moral foul-ups. We have sins of pride, greed, pornography, self-righteousness, lying, stealing, adultery, and insensitivity to others. But, through the power of Christ, there is hope for all of us. We want to expose these areas in our life, not deny them or rationalize them away. Not in a way that condemns, but in a way that transforms. We want to discover them, go to God for forgiveness, and become increasingly changed people.

It's messy, but beautiful.

Hypocrisy

As I mentioned earlier, I didn't become a Christ follower until I was a young adult (age twenty, in fact), but when I did, it was through some friends who invited me to a college outreach ministry. One of my early heroes, as you might imagine, was the president of that national campus movement. He was smart, disciplined, and a gifted teacher. I read his books, idolized his leadership, and even tried to model parts of my life after his. Then I got the opportunity to hear him speak at a conference. Not only that, but he and his wife were going to lead a breakout seminar on marriage designed for twentysomething singles who were just beginning to think about marriage for their own life. It was a smaller setting, so I got to see him and his wife up close and even ask some questions. It was everything I hoped it would be. I walked away more impressed and inspired than ever.

Then, just a few months later, the news broke. It came out that he had been in an affair with another woman. A several-months-long affair. As I did the math, to make matters even worse (for me), I realized he was still in that affair while he was leading that marriage seminar with his wife. The one I sat in and took notes on. The one where I was thinking, *This is who I want to be in my marriage.* The utter, sheer hypocrisy of it made me want to go find a corner in a room and vomit. I don't know if you've ever been burned like that or disillusioned like I was. It makes you question everything. But I didn't abandon the Christian faith. And though it wouldn't be the last time I experienced that disillusionment, I still haven't abandoned it. Because when I thought about it, I realized something very important. Just like with legalism or judgmentalism, hypocrisy doesn't have anything to do with *Jesus.* And Jesus went on the warpath against it. In fact, he's the one who started the war.

Have you ever seen masks like those known as comedy and tragedy in ancient Greece? There were actually all kinds of masks.

The masks of tragedy and comedy on display at Scarborough Hotel

In ancient Greek theater, actors wore masks that represented their character. Since all actors back then were male, it also allowed a male to play a female role. Do you know what the Greek word was for one of those actors? They were known as *hypocrites*. The art of the actor was that, from the moment he put on his mask, his entire conduct on stage would reflect the role. He was immersed in it. Obviously, for an actor, this is the goal.

Jesus took hold of this word and applied it to people who were *spiritual* actors. Here were some of his words:

> Everything they do is for show. . . .
>
> Hypocrites! For you are so careful to clean the outside of the cup and the dish, but inside you are filthy—full of greed and self-indulgence. (Matt. 23:5, 25 NLT)

He was just warming up. Here's more:

196

Hypocrites! . . . You pretend to be holy, with all your long, public prayers in the streets, while you are evicting widows from their homes. Hypocrites! . . .
You are like beautiful mausoleums—full of dead men's bones, and of foulness and corruption. You try to look like saintly men, but underneath those pious robes of yours are hearts besmirched with every sort of hypocrisy and sin. (Matt. 23:13–14, 27–28 TLB)

So what many people cite as a reason for rejecting Christianity and Christ has nothing to do with authentic Christian faith, much less Jesus. He was totally on board with despising it. Having said that, let's be equally clear about what hypocrisy *isn't*. Hypocrisy isn't when somebody falls below your expectation of perfection. It isn't catching someone who says they follow Jesus committing a sin. If that did define being a hypocrite, you'd have to add me to the list. Come spend a day with me and I will absolutely disappoint you. We probably wouldn't even last until 9:00 a.m. before chinks in my assumed-to-be-perfect armor began to show. So does that automatically make me a hypocrite? Just because I consistently fail at being like, living like, and acting like Jesus? Just because I screw up?

Just because I sin? So a Christian means . . . perfection? I certainly hope no one truly believes this. Yet the idea runs rampant, and not just among those who aren't Christians, but among those who are—or who would like to be. So many times I've heard someone say, "I don't want to say I'm a Christian . . ." or "I don't want to become a Christian . . ." or "I don't want to go to church as if I am a Christian . . ." or "I don't want to be baptized as a Christian . . ." And then it's always followed by, ". . . because I don't want to be a hypocrite."

Here's the thinking behind those statements: that being a Christ follower means being perfect, and being a hypocrite means saying you're a Christ follower and *not* being perfect. So since they don't want to be a hypocrite, they won't associate themselves with

Christians, the church, or Christ. But that is as screwed up as real hypocrisy is. The truth is that the opposite of hypocrisy is *not* perfection. The opposite of hypocrisy is spiritual *authenticity*. I fail a thousand times a day, but the real question is whether I'm more like Jesus now than I was five years ago. The Christian faith is unique in holding to the idea that the first step toward authentic spirituality is not about having your act together, but in knowing that you don't. This means an authentic Christian life isn't marked by perfection; it's marked by transformation.

C. S. Lewis once wrote about this in a way that I have found helpful. He said you may observe that a particular Christian woman you know (let's call her Mary) has a much more difficult time keeping away from gossip than a non-Christian woman that you know (let's call her Betty). So you see Mary the gossiping Christian and Betty the non-gossiping non-Christian. It naturally makes you think Mary is a hypocrite. Or that maybe the whole Christian-life "thing" doesn't have a lot of potency. But that misses the whole process of transformation. Here's the real issue: What would Mary be like if she were *not* in a relationship with Christ, and what would Betty be like if she *were*? We're all works in progress and have different areas of strengths and weaknesses. God meets every one of us where we are and begins there.

I remember once trying to describe this to a guy who was really into music and particularly liked the group Metallica. Metallica is a great band—one of the most successful rock bands of all time. Their third album, *Master of Puppets*, is often cited as one of the most influential albums in rock history. Their fifth album debuted at number one on the *Billboard* charts. So did their sixth, seventh, eighth, and ninth. In 2009, they were inducted into the Rock and Roll Hall of Fame. So I understood his interest in the band and appreciated it. One of their classic songs (and biggest hit to date) is "Enter Sandman." So I said to him, "Imagine a bunch of elementary school kids decide that they are going to tackle that song, and that they're going to perform it at a school fair for people who

Wikimedia Commons

Metallica on stage at the O2 Arena in London

had never heard 'Enter Sandman,' or anything else by Metallica, before. If those people hear the performance by that elementary school band, would it be fair or even reasonable for them to assess the worth of Metallica's music based on their performance?"

He said, "I don't know where you're going with this, but I'll play along. Those kids would butcher it! They're just kids! Their performance of it would have nothing to do with how good that song is, or how good a band Metallica is."

I said, "I agree. Now play that out spiritually. There are a lot of us Christians walking around trying to live for Jesus. But we're like elementary school kids in a garage band attempting to perform Metallica. Don't judge the composer or the music by those performances. Our failure at living the way Jesus lived has nothing to do with Jesus. Christians may disappoint you, but Jesus won't."

Intolerance

At this point, you may be saying, "Okay, I get the legalism, judgmentalism, and hypocrisy stuff. It's always bugged me, but it helps to know it bugged Jesus too. But what about basic things, like acceptance and tolerance? Actually, let me just cut to the chase: Are you accepting of gays? Because rumor has it you're not."

I've been asked that very question many, many times, and my answer has always been, "Of course! Why wouldn't we be?" There is no doubt that there have been Christians who, both in the past and even today, have been unloving and ungracious—even hateful—toward members of the LGBTQ community. But that lack of love is sin. God cares deeply about every human being on this planet—he loves them and wants to be in relationship with them.

Period.

Which means that every single person is welcome at an authentically Christian church. They will be accepted. They will be loved. They will be cared for. But here's where it gets tricky, and it's tricky for any number of lifestyles. If you want to make acceptance also mean affirmation, then that's a separate conversation that we're happy to have . . . but it's a separate conversation. Acceptance and affirmation are two different things. But regardless of whether the subsequent conversation plays out to everyone's liking, we will always accept, love, and care. The invitation is to figure out where you stand with Jesus and how he applies to your life. After you figure that out, you have to decide to either walk away from Christianity (which makes all other questions irrelevant) or to begin exploring what Jesus had to say about all kinds of things in our lives—including choices that we make about sex. Don't get this out of order, because there is no point in having this conversation until you settle where you stand with Jesus.

Let's say you're drawn to the idea of getting fit and losing weight. You hear about a fitness program that involves a high-protein/low-carb diet, coupled with a combination of cardio and strength-resistance training. You have a visceral reaction to the exclusion of carbs, because it seems intolerant, so you reject the entire plan. Wouldn't it be wiser to assess whether the plan itself works? If it does, perhaps you can reassess what it says about carbs. I know this is a weak analogy, as there is a significant difference between carbs and people. But let's play with the principle itself—namely, the importance we give to "tolerance." Today, being tolerant is a cardinal virtue. When you push people about what they mean by tolerance, they'll usually say things such as the importance of being accepting of others and respectful of their opinions and lifestyles. This, I would agree with. But push them even further, and you find that what they *really* mean is affirming all ideas, affirming all choices, and affirming all lifestyles as equally valid, true, and right. Here's where I have a problem. I'm not tolerant that way, and I really don't think you are either.

There are three kinds of tolerance. The first is *legal* tolerance. If you are an American, this has to do with your basic First Amendment right to believe what you want to believe. There is nothing in what Jesus says or that the Bible teaches that wars against such an idea. In fact, the Bible is a great advocate of legal tolerance.

The second kind of tolerance is *social* tolerance. This is accepting someone else as a human being regardless of what they believe, interacting with them in love, and exhibiting a relational openness to them as fellow human beings. There is nothing in the Christian faith that stands against this either. If Jesus stood for anything, it was open, loving acceptance of others as people who mattered to God. He was so well known for reaching out to those who were rejected in his day—the prostitutes, marketplace scoundrels, and thieves—that he was given the nickname the "friend of sinners." People didn't say that to be nice. It was basically a way of calling him a "son of a female dog"—I'll let your imagination fill in the earthier translation. It was a term of enormous derision. In the religious establishment of that day, if you spent time with a sinner that meant you were embracing their sin as well. In their minds, you were obviously *also* a prostitute or *also* a thief. They were ridiculing Jesus because he was so relationally accepting, even to the point of eating with these people in their homes.

In the ancient world, "table fellowship" was considered an act of intimacy—arguably among the closest of intimacies. This helps explain the depth of betrayal David felt when he spoke of those with whom he had shared bread, but who had then turned against him (Ps. 41); or the pain Jesus felt when his disciple Judas—immediately after taking the bread from his hand—went out into the night to claim his thirty pieces of silver for handing Jesus over to be arrested. To eat with anyone, and particularly a sinner, was far more than simply sharing a meal. It signified welcome, recognition, and acceptance. Dining with a sinner simply was not to be done—not even in the name of redemption. There was a rabbinic saying, "Let not a man associate with the wicked, even to bring him near to the law."[5] This is why we read of the shock and dismay of the religious establishment that Jesus was virtually indiscriminate with whom he ate. It was saying to the world, "This person is someone I value. This person is my friend." And this is the model for all who follow Jesus.

The third kind of tolerance is *intellectual* tolerance. This is accepting any and every idea as being equally valid, good, right, and true. And that's where Christianity draws a line. And I think, in truth, we all do. I remember being on a plane to Las Vegas, and a woman boarded in a sleeveless shirt with a huge tattoo on her shoulder that read "*F the World*." Only she had all four letters of the "F word" prominently on display. I fully support her legal right to have that tattoo. I would be happy to be in a loving and accepting relationship with her as a friend. But I absolutely don't agree with what she had inscribed on her body as a guiding life philosophy, and would actually enjoy the opportunity to tell her why. Later that same day, when I walked down the Vegas strip with my wife, there were lines of men wearing T-shirts that read "Girls delivered to your room in 20 minutes or less" and trying to hand me a little card with a picture of a naked woman and a phone number advertising an escort service. I don't embrace that as the optimal expression of God's design for my sexual fulfillment—neither for me, nor for the men and women involved. Is that being intolerant? Sure it is. Not socially, or legally, but intellectually. The point is that I don't believe that everything is equally right or equally valid. There is right and wrong, true and false, good and bad, smart and dumb. But isn't that where we all are? Do any of us really believe in intellectual tolerance? That all ideas are equally valid and should be treated as such? Of course not. If someone approached you and said, "I believe that the best way for you to have a great online experience is to remove your antivirus protection. Then open up every email attachment from people and companies you do not know, and download as much free software as you can from sites you have never heard of. Oh, and definitely respond to that email from that lawyer about that distant cousin of yours you didn't know existed from Nigeria who only needs your bank account and Social Security number to give you your million-dollar inheritance." You could easily be tolerant of that person legally and relationally, while reasonably rejecting what he says about the way to handle yourself online.

When we talk about the importance of tolerance, we mean legal tolerance or social tolerance but not intellectual tolerance. Let's bring this back to spiritual things. When Jesus said things like he was *the* way, *the* truth, and *the* life, it wasn't simply a declaration—it was an invitation. He wasn't refusing anyone their right to believe differently, much less rejecting anyone socially or culturally. Jesus was just saying, "I am the way to know God as Father! There's one God and one way! There is a God, and he's not confused about who he is and what he stands for and what is true, and right and wrong. And I am here to make it foundationally and fundamentally clear." This is true for lifestyle issues as well. If the only kind of acceptance you will allow involves uncritical affirmation, then you are saying the only kind of tolerance you will accept includes intellectual tolerance. This would mean that any and every lifestyle choice must be affirmed as equally good and safe and vibrant and fulfilling and holy as any other. Can't you think of at least one lifestyle practice that you would personally reject, not just for you but for everyone? Christianity walks a fine but important line, as most of us do, on any number of lifestyle issues in relation to the people involved in light of legal, relational, and intellectual tolerance. It's a line bathed in both grace and truth, just as is true of the entire Christian message.

Sexism

On October 15, 2017, when the actress Alyssa Milano sent out a tweet that said, "If you've been sexually harassed or assaulted write 'me too' as a reply to this tweet," she woke up the next day to find that more than 30,000 people had used the hashtag #MeToo. Within twenty-four hours, it had risen to 12 million. Now, #MeToo has been used millions of times in at least eighty-five countries. It has resulted in a very public reckoning as women have been emboldened and empowered to come forward. *Time* magazine says that the #MeToo movement has unleashed one of the highest-velocity shifts in our culture since the 1960s. In their article on naming the "silence breakers" their Person of the Year, they wrote:

> Women have had it with bosses and co-workers who not only cross boundaries but don't even seem to know that boundaries exist. They've had it with the fear of retaliation, or being blackballed, of being fired from a job they can't afford to lose. They've had it with the code of going along to get along. They've had it with men who use their power to take what they want from women. . . . [And so they have] started a revolution.[6]

The classic definition of *sexism* is the economic exploitation and/or social domination of members of one sex by another. And specifically, of women by men. It's when women are discriminated against—when they are stereotyped, when there is prejudice—just

Series graphic from Mecklenburg Community Church

because they are women. Misogyny, or having a misogynistic attitude or being misogynous in your behavior, all relates to having a negative attitude toward women. The word *misogynist* literally means someone who is a hater of women. What is disturbing, in the minds of many, is the perception that the Christian faith is deeply sexist.

Is it true?

While the Bible doesn't flinch from recording the sexual misdeeds of the men and women in its stories, it doesn't flinch from its denunciation of them either. There is no place in God's economy for sexual harassment, assault, or rape. There is no place for using positions of power or influence to coerce or pressure for sexual favors. And the call to how we should interact with people of the opposite sex—as men—on a daily basis, is also clear. When the apostle Paul wrote to Timothy as his mentor in life and leadership, he said, "Treat . . . older women as mothers, and younger women as sisters, with absolute purity" (1 Tim. 5:1–2).

But what of women being seen as inferior to men? Again, this is often assumed to be part of the fabric of the Christian faith. The truth is you can't get past the opening page of the Bible without things related to sexism being denounced and God making it very clear that it has no place in our lives. Consider the creation narrative itself. In the opening pages of the first book of the Bible, the book of Genesis, you read these words:

> Then God said, "Let us make mankind in our image, in our likeness, so that they may rule over the fish in the sea and the birds in the sky, over the livestock and all the wild animals, and over all the creatures that move along the ground."
>
> So God created man in his own image,
>   in the image of God he created them;
>   male and female he created them. (Gen. 1:26–27)

When God created mankind, he made us male and female. And both were made, equally, in the image of God. There's not more of the image of God in one than the other. And we were given a *mutual* charge to steward the world. Which means there is not an ounce of sexism in what God created, how God created, or the intent of God's creation of us as men and women. When sexism became entrenched due to our sinful natures, God wasted no time in addressing its fundamental disorder. Supremely, through the coming of Jesus to earth. During the time of Jesus, sexism ran rampant. Let me give you a picture of how devalued women were in the Greco-Roman world. If a couple had a baby girl, they had the option to discard her simply because she was a girl. People wanted sons, so if they had a daughter they could just put the baby girl on the doorstep. Then people would come around and take these infant girls and raise them up to be slaves or prostitutes. There was even a prayer in which Jewish men thanked God that they were not a slave, a Gentile, or a woman.

Women were treated as mere objects that could be used for work and sexual fulfillment, and then divorced in a heartbeat without any penalty or societal concern. A man could get a divorce from his wife for anything from a badly cooked meal to the mere fact that he found her less beautiful than another woman. And then he could remarry at will and leave her—much like the baby girl on the doorstep—to fend for herself without any support or any hope. Jesus didn't treat women that way. He didn't view women that way. He invited them to follow him and be among his burgeoning church. He treated them with respect and honor and enormous sensitivity. And he made it clear that they were anything but second-class citizens. Do you remember our conversation about Mary in the chapter on the resurrection? How she was the first person he appeared to following his resurrection, and he gave her the charge of telling his male followers that he had indeed risen from the dead? That was a cultural bombshell. The Bible records that the first witness to Jesus after he was raised from the dead was a woman! And not only the first witness, but the one person Jesus tasked to go and tell all the *men* what happened. In the ancient Near Eastern culture of that day, women were extremely low on the societal totem pole. So low that their testimony was not accepted in the Jewish courts of law. Even if multiple women were eyewitnesses of the same event, their testimony was not accepted. Yet Jesus purposefully went, first, to a woman and chose her to be his eyewitness. And not simply to other women, but to men! He could have appeared to anyone, tasked anyone; he purposefully chose Mary. In other words, he purposefully chose to take a baseball bat to any and all sexism. He purposefully and powerfully dictated that sexism had no place in his kingdom. Jesus radically affirmed the full dignity of women and the value of their witness and role in the life of the revolution he came to unleash. From the very first moments of the early Christian church, the unheard of took root right away: women were involved and treated as equals. Men and women may have different roles, different responsibilities, but they are on completely equal footing before God. In the New Testament we find them speaking in the church, teaching in the church, helping to provide leadership to the church, with church groups meeting in their homes. Names such as Phoebe and Priscilla, Mary and Martha, became as prominent as any man's.

So let's close this conversation with what I hope is now clear. Judgmentalism, legalism, hypocrisy, intolerance, and sexism are, in truth, not part of the Christian world. At least, not the world (much less church) Jesus came to establish. They manifest themselves as part of the sin-stained, sin-soaked nature of all of humanity, Christ followers included, but they are not endemic to the Christian faith. They are precisely what the Christian faith seeks to eradicate from every human life and every human community.

8

NEXT STEPS

I shall be telling this with a sigh
Somewhere ages and ages hence:
Two roads diverged in a wood, and I—
I took the one less traveled by,
And that has made all the difference.

Robert Frost,
"The Road Not Taken," 1916

We've come to the end of our time together. I've tried to not only explain Christianity but to make a case for it. I don't know where you're at with it all at this point, but I would like to offer some suggestions. I'm going to throw out a few scenarios and what I would encourage you to consider pursuing as possible next steps in light of each one.

Deal Breakers

The first scenario occurs when you feel as though the Christian faith has a deal breaker or two that you just can't get past. So in terms of continuing to explore or even consider the Christian faith, you're thinking, *I probably shouldn't even bother. I know there is [this issue] that I can't get past.* Should you bother to continue? I would say, "Absolutely. Yes!" And here's why. You may find that what you *think* Christianity maintains in a particular area isn't what it maintains at all. You may have some misconceptions floating around that are caricatures of the Christian faith. You may think you're not in agreement with the Christian faith in areas where you actually are. Even if there are some sticking points for you, consider this: if you go into exploring mode and become convinced down the road that there is a God, and he has made himself and the truth about himself known, then how are you going to feel about the disagreements you thought you had with him and his truth on the front end? Won't you be so glad you didn't let that stop you?

But there's more. If you want the Christian faith to line up 100 percent with your current ideas and ideals and then—and only then—will you accept it, you don't want God. You want a mirror, because you have established yourself as God. The heart of the Christian faith is realizing that you are not God, and neither am I. This means that coming to God will involve—no matter who you are or what you currently believe—bending a knee. Two, to be exact. There is much you might chafe against but, in the end, the call is to submit your will to his. This means a strategic part of your journey will inevitably involve taking on an entirely new evaluative paradigm based not on your own understanding, but on God's.

Changes

The next scenario you may find yourself in is realizing only too well that becoming a follower of Christ will mean making changes, and you don't want to change. I get it. There was a moment—just a moment—before I got engaged when I thought, *What in the world am I doing?!* Because in that moment I thought of all the things I'd be giving up or changing . . . *forever*. Like dating. Dating was . . . like . . . the best! Never again would I be able to see an attractive, appealing woman and have the freedom to pursue the relationship. That's not all. Once married, I would probably have to fold my underwear, screw the top back on the toothpaste, put my dirty clothes in a basket, and spend my weekends going to fabric stores. I thought I wouldn't be able to go out with my friends, stay out all night, or take off on a skiing trip. And what if I couldn't keep it up? I was thinking about it like a lifelong diet, and who wants that? So for a moment—just a moment—I remember panicking and becoming very unsure about whether this was such a smart thing to do.

At the time of this writing, that was thirty-seven years ago. Now I look back and think, *What an idiot I was! I was worried about what I would have lost? What was I thinking?* Why? Because now I know what I've gained. Now I cannot imagine life apart from my wife. What I have experienced over the years of my marriage *far* outweighs *anything* I may have imagined I was going to sacrifice by entering into that commitment. I am not less of a person, but more of a person. I don't have less of a life, I have more of a life. My wife, my children, my grandchildren, our love, our relationship, our memories, our support, our encouragement, our loyalty, our laughter . . . is the heartbeat of my life!

Did it take making changes? Yes. Did it take making a commitment? Yes. Making a spiritual commitment *is* a similar commitment to marriage. It's a life-changer. And the heart of that change is a committed relationship with God through Christ. It starts by trusting him as your Savior and knowing that your relationship with him is secure—forever. Nothing will ever change that. Then as you walk with him, he in his grace will help you month by month to take out of your life what should not be there and put in what should be there. It's okay to be nervous about entering into that relationship on the front end. If you weren't a little nervous, I would question whether you understood the nature of the decision.

I remember like it was yesterday how I felt when I was weighing all of this out for my life. I felt like I did before I got married. I remember talking to a Christian friend of mine on the very night I did cross the line, repeating, "But there's so much that will have to change! I mean, so much that will have to change!" And I was right. It was a complete reorientation of my values, a complete reorientation of my priorities. And it scared me. But you know what I finally got? That this was the point! I was being invited into life change. But wasn't that what I longed for? I was being invited into life change but, like with my marriage, it became more than that—I was being invited into life itself. I just didn't know how dead I was before. But I do now. Without a doubt, my relationship with Jesus is the best thing that has ever happened to me.

C. S. Lewis once wrote that this hesitancy to make the decision to trust Jesus as our Savior and grow as a Christian is like a child who lives in the slums and has only known playing in a running sewage, open water, dirty mudhole, having no idea what it means to have a vacation at the sea.[1]

Oh, and please don't let this idea of "But I don't know if I can keep it up" be a barrier for you. I can go ahead and tell you right now that you won't be able to keep it up. None of us can. It's not about "keeping it up" but "keeping it real." Again, it's like a marriage—there will be highs and lows; seasons that are golden followed by "fight nights" you wouldn't believe. The goal is to stay in the game, what Eugene Peterson calls a "long obedience in the same direction." It will often feel like you're taking three steps forward, followed by two steps backward. But you're on the journey, and that's the goal.

Line Crossing

On to the next scenario. What do you do if you realize you're seriously thinking about accepting all of this? *I'm finding myself believing . . . being drawn to Jesus and the Christian faith. Which kind of surprises even me. I know that means crossing a line. But I'm not sure what that line is and, if I'm honest, I'm not sure I'm ready to cross it. So I have a bunch of "now what" kinds of questions about that.*

Fair enough. Let's begin with what it means to become a "believer." First, it doesn't mean that you have all your questions answered. Does that surprise you? Whenever we make a decision about something, most of us want to be sure, beyond any doubt, of what is absolutely true. That will never happen spiritually. We're talking about God, and there is no way you can get every question about him answered. If you could fathom everything that there is to know about God, he'd be no bigger than your mind—no larger than your intellect—and that would be a small God. The goal isn't to get *every* answer, but *enough* answers. The line of faith can be reasonably and responsibly crossed when you come to the point that you realize it takes more faith *not* to believe in the claims of Christ than *to* believe in the claims of Christ.

Let's say you're beyond the reasonable-doubt stage. Let's say you still have some lingering questions about some things (like the rest of us), but you're much more of a believer than a nonbeliever. It would take more for you to walk away at this point than to stay. So what then?

The next step is to realize that belief is where a relationship with Christ begins. This belief is more than intellectual assent. It's believing that there is a God, that the Bible is his Word to us, that Jesus was who he said he was—God himself in human form sent to earth to show us the way to be in relationship with God as Father. But belief is not enough. You have to place your trust in Christ alone as your only way to God, your only way to live forever. The word *believe* in the original Greek is *pisteuo*. It means to be convinced of something, to trust. You come to God as a sinner, recognize Christ died for you and rose again, and place your trust in Christ alone to save you. Not Christ *plus* anything you have done but Christ alone as your only way to God, your only way to heaven. The moment you trust him brings you into an eternal relationship with him. When you're open to that, then you're ready for what comes next: crossing the line.

The Bridge

How do we cross the line into a relationship with God through Jesus? The Bible says to think of it like a bridge: "God is on one side and all the people [are] on the other side, and Christ Jesus . . . is between them to bring them together, by giving his life for all mankind" (1 Tim. 2:5–6 TLB). Let me sketch that out a bit, reviewing some ground we've already covered, beginning with the reality that God made us and loves us and wants to be in relationship with us.[2] But we rebelled against God, disobeyed him, and went our own way, and that separated us from him and broke off the relationship. It created this giant chasm between us and God.

US   GOD

Now, there are a lot of ways people have tried to repair this when they sense their spiritual condition. They want to figure out how to cross over, to get back to God, to restore the relationship, to bridge the gap. Some people try to earn it, work for it; they tally up points toward it by doing good deeds, going to church, obeying the law, and so on.

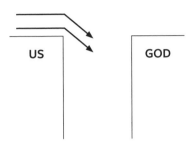

But those are not what get you to God. Because, according to the Bible, good works can't bridge the gap. Nothing will ever be enough. It all falls short. So we can't ever be good enough, right enough, *anything* enough, to bridge this gap between us and God. And, to raise the stakes even further, there is a penalty for our sins, and that penalty is death. The Bible says, "For the wages of sin is death" (Rom. 6:23).

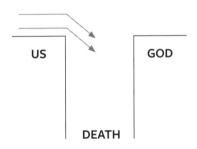

So there really is a problem. There really is an issue that needs to be addressed in our life, and it's not one we can fix on our own. It's not about the degree to which you are a sinner, or the amount of sin in your life. The wages of sin is simply death. And there's no amount of good works even possible to offset it. There's not a different set of wages we can earn to balance the books. But there's a second half to the verse we read a moment ago: "For the wages of sin is death, *but* the gift of God is eternal life in Christ Jesus our Lord" (Rom. 6:23, emphasis added). Our sin separates us from God and, unless somehow addressed, the separation remains in place. But—and this is important—God loves us so much that he has provided a bridge over which we can find full forgiveness and the full restoration of our relationship with him. Christ paid the penalty for our sin in full through his death on the cross, thus wiping out death and providing the bridge we need.

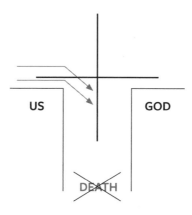

But you can't stop there. Just knowing about the cross and what it can do for your life is not enough. The Bible teaches that you must act upon it, accept it, receive the gift of the cross. You have to *cross over*. You have to walk across the bridge that has been provided.

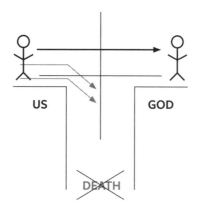

Think of it this way. Imagine I'm holding a box in my hands, a wrapped gift with a tag that has your name on it. If I were to come to you and say, "Do you see this tag? It has your name on it and I bought this for you. It is my gift to you. You don't have to pay for it—it's my gift to you." And then I hold it out to you in my hand. When is it actually yours? *When you take it.* I can stand there and hold it out to you all day long; it's not yours until you reach out and accept that gift. This is why walking across the bridge—taking that gift—is *everything.*

So where are you in reference to this bridge? Are you way far away from it, still tire-kicking Christianity? Or are you right at the bridge, right at the cross, and you know there's only one thing left for you to do—either reject the whole thing or walk over it?

And you don't want to reject it.

If it's the latter, why not tell God in prayer what you are doing? Please understand, saying a prayer doesn't save anybody. You are not saved through praying; you are saved through trusting Christ. You are forever his the moment you trust Christ alone as your personal Savior. But verbalizing this in prayer can be very helpful because although God knows what you are doing— trusting Christ—expressing it in prayer cements it in your own mind.

This brings us to the prayer itself.

If you can admit where you stand before a holy God, if you can acknowledge that you believe Jesus has provided the only way to be saved, then you can reach out and receive the gift of what Christ did for you through his death on the cross.

Here's the kind of prayer you can use. Begin by saying to God, in your own words, that you need him. You have been living in a way that is far from him. You are a sinner who is in need of a Savior.

Then tell him you want to be forgiven for your sins. You want a clean slate, a new beginning, your past erased. You know what

Christ did on the cross applies to you, and you believe. Your prayer might sound something like this:

Dear God, I know I am a sinner. I am separated from you. I also know that sin must be punished. I now believe that Jesus Christ took that punishment when he died in my place on a cross and rose again. Right now, I trust Jesus alone as my Savior. Thank you for accepting me and for the forgiveness and eternal life I now have.

If or when you pray that prayer, may I give you a quick "pastoral word"? When you're ready, tell somebody; let someone know. Maybe the person who gave you this book. Maybe a friend or family member. Just let someone know. And then find a church. Remember, our faith is not supposed to exist in a vacuum. Find a community of believers to do life with and grow with.

Please tell somebody so they can pray for you, encourage you, help you take next steps in the relationship. But make no mistake: you've answered the question the way Jesus hoped you would, and nothing will ever be the same in your life.

I want to be the first to say, "Welcome home."

Now That You've Crossed the Bridge

Salvation is not the stopping point; it is the starting point. God has just saved you, now he wants to lead you. There is nobody better to do that than him. After all, he is the one who made you, knows you, and gifted you with particular abilities. As exciting as it is to come to Christ, it is even more exciting to grow as a Christian.

So day by day ask him to have the leadership in your life. Let him know that you welcome his day-in, day-out management of your life and that you want to live your life under his direction, realizing that you will make mistakes along the way. Let him know that you want to find out how he wants you to live. As I mentioned earlier, in love, grace, kindness, and understanding, he will help take out of your life what should not be there and put in what should be there. You will not regret trusting Jesus; you may regret that you did not do it sooner.

Once again, welcome home and welcome to a new life!

NOTES

Introduction

1. Os Guinness, *In Two Minds: The Dilemma of Doubt and How to Resolve It* (Downers Grove, IL: InterVarsity, 1976), 24–25.

2. There are many biographies available on Lewis, including Roger Lancelyn Green and Walter Hooper, *C. S. Lewis: A Biography*, rev. ed. (New York: Harvest, 1994); Alan Jacobs, *The Narnian: The Life and Imagination of C. S. Lewis* (New York: Harper, 2005); David C. Downing, *The Most Reluctant Convert: C. S. Lewis's Journey to Faith* (Downers Grove, IL: InterVarsity, 2002); George Sayer, *Jack: C. S. Lewis and His Times* (New York: Harper & Row, 1988); Humphrey Carpenter, *The Inklings* (New York: Ballantine, 1978); and Lewis's own spiritual autobiography, *Surprised by Joy* (New York: Harvest, 1955).

3. Lewis, *Surprised by Joy*, 228–29.

4. I caution that these were tales told to me while in Oxford by those who claimed to have known and interacted with Lewis. But from all that I know and have read, I would tend to lean on the side of their truth. For example, when the *Daily Telegraph* referred to Lewis as an ascetic, Tolkien wrote to his son, "'Ascetic Mr. Lewis'—!!! I ask you! He put away three pints in a very short session we had this morning, and said he was 'going short for Lent.'" Jacobs, *Narnian*, 190.

5. Adapted from Carpenter, *The Inklings*, 45–48, as well as my own journeys to Oxford and dialogues with Oxford folk.

Chapter 1 The God Who Is There . . . or Not

1. "When Americans Say They Believe in God, What Do They Mean?" Pew Research Center, April 25, 2018, http://www.pewforum.org/2018/04/25/when-americans-say-they-believe-in-god-what-do-they-mean/.

2. Carl Sagan, *Cosmos* (New York: Random House, 1980), 4.

3. As noted by Fred Heeren in *Show Me God: What the Message from Space Is Telling Us About God* (Wheeling, IL: Searchlight Publications, 1995), 139. Smoot's quote was cited by Milton Rothman, "What Went Before?" *Free Inquiry* 13, no. 1 (Winter 1992/93): 12.

4. Robert Jastrow, *God and the Astronomers*, 2nd ed. (New York: W. W. Norton, 1992), 14.

5. Jastrow, *God and the Astronomers*, 107.

6. On this, see Neil deGrasse Tyson, *Astrophysics for People in a Hurry* (New York: W. W. Norton, 2017), 26.

7. Plato believed that "the order of the motion of stars . . . [would] lead men to believe in the gods" (*Laws* 12.966e).

8. "Top 10 Incredibly Advanced Fighter Jets in 2017," AviationCV.com, May 19, 2017, https://www.aviationcv.com/aviation-blog/2017/top-10-fighter-jets-world-2017.

9. Tyson, *Astrophysics,* 78.

10. Tyson, *Astrophysics*, 176.

11. Tyson, *Astrophysics*, 30.

12. As cited by Luis Palau, *God Is Relevant* (New York: Doubleday, 1997), 32.

13. Paul Davies, *The Mind of God* (New York: Simon & Schuster, 1992), 232. Even if life on another planet, such as Mars, is verified, the miraculous origin of life is not diminished, for nowhere does the Bible intimate that God created life on this planet alone.

14. Stephen Hawking, quoted by John Boslough, *Masters of Time—Cosmology at the End of Innocence* (New York: Addison-Wesley Publishing Company, 1992), 55.

15. Stephen Hawking, *A Brief History of Time* (New York: Bantam Books, 1988), 127.

16. On this, see George Marsden, *Fundamentalism and American Culture: The Shaping of Twentieth-Century Evangelicalism 1870–1925* (Oxford: Oxford University Press, 1980), particularly 184–88.

17. Unknown origin, but adapted from John Ortberg's contribution to *How I Changed My Mind about Evolution*, ed. Kathryn Applegate and J. B. Stump (Downers Grove, IL: InterVarsity, 2016), 92.

18. Nadia Whitehead, "Origins Opinion Surveys Evolve from 'How' to 'Who,'" *Christianity Today*, February 12, 2019, https://www.christianitytoday.com/ct/20 18/january-web-only/christian-origins-surveys-evolve-from-how-to-who.html.

19. Devleena Mani Tiwari, "Origin and Evolution of Life on Earth," Science India, accessed August 2018, http://scienceindia.in/home/view_article/368.

20. Sir Fred Hoyle, *The Intelligent Universe* (London: Michael Joseph, 1983), 11–12, 19, 251. I am indebted to Hoyle for the inspiration for the F-22 illustration.

21. Fred Hoyle and Chandra Wickramasinghe, *Evolution from Space* (London: J. M. Dent and Sons, 1981), 24.

22. Charles Darwin, *On the Origin of Species by Means of Natural Selection*, ed. Joseph Carroll (Ontario, Canada: Broadview Press, 2003), 213.

23. Michael J. Behe, *Darwin's Black Box: The Biochemical Challenge to Evolution* (New York: Free Press, 1996), 42–48. See also his later work, *The Edge of Evolution: The Search for the Limits of Darwinism* (New York: Free Press, 2007).

24. Further, mutation cannot account for such development either, for while mutation can cause variation on a theme, it cannot produce an altogether different "thing." For example, Behe gives the following analogy: "A mutation is a change in *one* of the lines of instructions. So instead of saying, 'Take a 1/4-inch nut' a mutation might say, 'Take a 3/8-inch nut.' . . . What a mutation *cannot* do is change all the instructions in one step—say, to build a fax machine instead of a radio." Behe, *Darwin's Black Box*, 41. Intriguingly, Darwin himself noted that "To suppose that the eye with all its inimitable contrivances for adjusting the focus to different distances, for admitting different amounts of light, and for the correction of spherical and chromatic aberration, could have been formed by natural selection, seems, I freely confess, absurd in the highest degree." See Darwin, *On the Origin of Species*, 211.

25. Behe, *Darwin's Black Box*, 232. On intelligent design, see Douglas Axe, *Undeniable: How Biology Confirms Our Intuition that Life Is Designed* (New York: HarperOne, 2016); William Dembski, *The Design Revolution* (Downers Grove, IL: InterVarsity, 2004); Stephen C. Meyer, *Signature in the Cell: DNA and the Evidence for Intelligent Design* (New York: HarperOne, 2009).

26. Julie Borg, "Evolutionary Scientist Admits Theory's Major Flaws," *Baptist Press*, September 8, 2017, http://bpnews.net/49504/evolutionary-scientist-admits -theorys-major-flaws.

27. Applegate and Stump, eds., *How I Changed My Mind about Evolution*, 94.

28. The idea dates at least as far back as Ludwig Feuerbach in the 1830s but was popularized by Sigmund Freud in *The Future of an Illusion* in *Complete Psychological Works*, 24 vols. (London: Hogarth, 1953), vol. 21. Many have noted that Freud's ideas come more from his own atheistic prejudices than hard experimental evidence from his own discipline.

29. Sarah Knapton, "Everyone Everywhere Shares Seven Universal Moral Rules, Oxford University Finds," *The Telegraph*, February 8, 2019, https://www.tele graph.co.uk/science/2019/02/08/everyone-everywhere-shares-common-moral -code-oxford-university/.

30. On this, see C. S. Lewis, *Mere Christianity* (New York: Macmillan, 1952), 3–7. For a detailed discussion, see Basil Mitchell, *Morality: Secular and Religious* (Oxford: Clarendon, 1980), as well as Immanuel Kant, *Critique of Practical Reason*.

31. Lewis, *Mere Christianity*, 31.

32. As cited by Palau, *God Is Relevant*, 182.

33. Marcelo Gleiser, "The 10 Most Important Questions in Science," NPR, September 13, 2013, http://www.npr.org/blogs/13.7/2013/09/10/221019045/the-10 -most-important-questions-in-science; Hayley Birch, Colin Stuart, and Mun Keat Looi, "The 20 Big Questions in Science," *The Guardian*, August 31, 2013, http:// www.theguardian.com/science/2013/sep/01/20-big-questions-in-science.

34. Francis Collins, as quoted in Applegate and Stump, eds., *How I Changed My Mind about Evolution*, 71. See also Collins's earlier book, *The Language of God: A Scientist Presents Evidence for Belief* (New York: Free Press, 2006), particularly the third chapter.

35. Lewis, *Mere Christianity*, 66.

Chapter 2 But What Kind of God?

1. As cited by Philip Yancey, *The Jesus I Never Knew* (Grand Rapids: Zondervan, 1995), 264. For a helpful biblical and theological introduction to the Christian understanding of God, see J. I. Packer, *Knowing God* (Downers Grove, IL: InterVarsity, 1973).

2. This blog entry was posted at http.//www.mwillett.org/atheism/If_I_Was_God.htm, accessed September 2009; however, it has since been taken down.

3. As cited by Philip Yancey, *Disappointment with God* (Grand Rapids: Zondervan, 1988), 179.

4. C. S. Lewis, *A Grief Observed* (San Francisco: Harper & Row, 1961), 10–11.

5. Langdon Gilkey, *Shantung Compound* (New York: HarperSanFrancisco, 1966/1975), 115–16.

6. As cited by Cornelius Plantinga Jr., *Not the Way It's Supposed to Be: A Breviary of Sin* (Grand Rapids: Eerdmans, 1995), 7.

7. Philip Yancey, *Where Is God When It Hurts?* (Grand Rapids: Zondervan/ Campus Life, 1990), 61, 69.

8. Boethius, *The Consolation of Philosophy*, translated with an introduction by V. E. Watts (New York: Penguin, 1969), 125.

9. This is widely attributed to Chesterton without protest, is widely considered to be the basis for his 1910 work *What's Wrong with the World*, and has never been attributed to anyone else. Chestertonians consider it valid and reflective of his humility and wit (see the official website of the American Chesterton Society at chesterton.org), but alas, there is no documentary evidence.

10. Philip Yancey, *Reaching for the Invisible God* (Grand Rapids: Zondervan, 2000), 56–57.

11. Will and Ariel Durant, *The Lessons of History* (New York: Simon & Schuster, 1968), 81.

12. James Dobson, *When God Doesn't Make Sense* (Wheaton: Tyndale, 1993), 193.

13. David Van Biema, "When God Hides His Face," *Time Magazine*, July 8, 2001, http://content.time.com/time/magazine/article/0,9171,166728-3,00.html.

14. C. S. Lewis, *The Problem of Pain* (New York: HarperCollins, 1996), 22. Not only is there the "good" of free will, but there can be a positive element to pain. Lewis called it the "megaphone of God" that arrests our attention; Dr. Paul Brand applauds its benefits for physical defense and as an early-warning system to our bodies; James Dobson and Philip Yancey note its use for faith-development. But it must never be seen, in and of itself, as *good*: only as able to be used by God for good in spite of its tragic nature.

15. C. S. Lewis, *The Four Loves* (New York: Harcourt, Brace, 1960), 121.

16. Philip Yancey, *What's So Amazing About Grace?* (Grand Rapids: Zondervan, 1997), 56.

17. As cited by Billy Graham, *Hope for the Troubled Heart* (Dallas: Word, 1991), 44–45.

18. Frederick Buechner, *Wishful Thinking* (New York: Harper & Row, 1973), 17.

19. See Craig Brian Lawson, *Illustrations for Preaching and Teaching from Leadership Journal* (Grand Rapids: Baker, 1999), 210.

20. Richard Dawkins, *The God Delusion* (New York: Houghton Mifflin, 2006), 51.

21. For example, Walter A. Elwell, ed., *Baker Encyclopedia of the Bible*, vol. 1 (Grand Rapids: Baker, 1997), 409.

22. On this, see Paul Copan, *Is God a Moral Monster? Making Sense of the Old Testament* (Grand Rapids: Baker Books, 2011).

23. Miroslav Volf, *Free of Charge: Giving and Forgiving in a Culture Stripped of Grace* (Grand Rapids: Zondervan, 2005), 138–39, emphasis original.

Chapter 3 Jesus 101

1. Yancey, *Jesus I Never Knew*, 17.

2. For a good article on this, read Rebecca McLaughlin, "How to Defend the Gospels with Confidence," *Christianity Today*, January 7, 2019, https://www.christianitytoday.com/ct/2019/january-web-only/peter-williams-can-we-trust-gospels.html.

3. Mike Fillon, "The Real Face of Jesus," *Esquire*, December 11, 2015, https://www.esquire.com/lifestyle/a40399/jesus-real-face/.

4. Yancey, *Jesus I Never Knew*, 36.

5. Max Lucado, *God Came Near* (Nashville: Thomas Nelson, 2004), 25–26, emphasis original.

6. While there is much debate about the age of Joseph at the time of his engagement to Mary, there are writings that are inclined to support this given the maturity and wisdom he exercised in response to everything associated with the virgin birth. See Fr. Maurice Meschler, SJ, *The Truth about Saint Joseph: Encountering the Most Hidden of Saints* (Manchester, NH: Sophia Institute Press, 2017), as well as *Protoevangelium of James*, an apocryphal gospel.

7. Arial Sabar, "Karen King Responds to 'The Unbelievable Tale of Jesus's Wife,'" *The Atlantic*, June 16, 2016, https://www.theatlantic.com/politics/archive/2016/06/karen-king-responds-to-the-unbelievable-tale-of-jesus-wife/487484/.

8. J. T. Fisher and L. S. Hawley, *A Few Buttons Missing* (Philadelphia: Lippincott, 1951), 273.

9. Lewis, *Mere Christianity*, 40–41.

10. Brent Curtis and John Eldredge, *The Sacred Romance* (Nashville: Thomas Nelson, 1997), 73.

11. Curtis and Eldredge, *The Sacred Romance*, 74.

12. Søren Kierkegaard, *Philosophical Fragments*, taken from *A Kierkegaard Anthology*, ed. Robert Bretall (Princeton: Princeton University Press, 1946), 165–66.

13. This was adapted from Lee Strobel, *The Case for Miracles* (Grand Rapids: Zondervan, 2018). The investigative principles Warner followed were taken from Warner's book, *Cold-Case Christianity* (Colorado Springs: David C. Cook, 2013).

14. Eusebius, for example, records the martyrdom of Peter; James, the brother of Jesus; and James, the brother of John.

15. On the traditions surrounding their deaths, see *Foxe's Book of Martyrs*.

16. On the medical evidence that Jesus truly died as a result of his ordeal, see William D. Edwards, Wesley J. Gabel, and Floyd E. Hosmer, "On the Physical

Death of Jesus Christ," *Journal of the American Medical Association* 255, no. 11 (March 21, 1986): 1463.

17. N. T. Wright, *The Resurrection of the Son of God: Christian Origins and the Question of God*, vol. 3 (Minneapolis: Fortress, 2003), 707.

18. Søren Kierkegaard, *Either/Or: A Fragment of Life* (United Kingdom: Penguin Random House, 1992), 131.

Chapter 4 The Message

1. Will D. Campbell, *Brother to a Dragonfly* (New York: Continuum, 1987), 220.

2. Brennan Manning, *The Ragamuffin Gospel* (Colorado Springs: Multnomah, 2005), 11.

3. Manning, *Ragamuffin Gospel*, 49.

4. Henry Cloud, *Changes That Heal* (Grand Rapids: Zondervan, 2018).

5. Adapted from Yancey, *What's So Amazing About Grace?*

6. "Fact: There are 80,000 Ways to Drink a Starbucks Beverage," *Huffington Post*, March 4, 2014, http://www.huffingtonpost.com/2014/03/04/starbucks_n _4890735.html.

7. Lewis, *Mere Christianity*, 35.

8. Josh Voorhees, "The List of Who People Trust Less Than a Congressman Is a Short One," *Slate*, Dec. 3, 2012, http://www.slate.com/blogs/the_slatest /2012/12/03/gallup_trustworthy_poll_congressmen_car_salesman_least_trusted _professions.html.

9. As quoted by Durant and Durant, *Lessons of History*, 51.

10. Penn Jillette, "Penn Says: A Gift of a Bible," *Crackle*, December 8, 2008, accessed March 26, 2009, http://crackle.com/c/Penn_Says/A_Gift_of_a_Bible/2415037. Now found on YouTube at https://www.youtube.com/watch?v=6md638smQd8.

11. For an overview of the correspondence theory of truth, see A. N. Prior, "Correspondence Theory of Truth," *The Encyclopedia of Philosophy*, ed. Paul Edwards (New York: Macmillan Publishing Co., Inc. and The Free Press, 1967), vol. 2, 223–32; on the concept of truth in the Bible, see Anthony C. Thisleton, "Truth," *The New International Dictionary of New Testament Theology*, vol. 3, ed. Colin Brown (Grand Rapids: Regency/Zondervan, 1986), 874–902; the classical understanding of the correspondence theory of truth can be found in the writings of Aristotle, such as "Metaphysica," trans. W. D. Ross, *The Great Books of the Western World*, vol. 8, ed. Robert Maynard Hutchins (Chicago: Encyclopaedia Britannica, Inc., 1952), 1011.b.26ff., "Categoriae," trans. E. M. Edghill, *The Great Books of the Western World*, vol. 8, ed. Robert Maynard Hutchins (Chicago: Encyclopaedia Britannica, Inc., 1952), 4.a.10–4.b.19, and "De interpretatione," trans. E. M. Edghill, *The Great Books of the Western World*, vol. 8, ed. Robert Maynard Hutchins (Chicago: Encyclopaedia Britannica, Inc., 1952), 16.a.10–19.

12. Unless, of course, you want to deny the reliability of our senses and posit that we are removed from any understanding of true reality. This, however, leads to nothing but intellectual nihilism. For a full treatment of the concept of truth in contemporary American evangelical Christian thought, see the author's *What Is Truth?* (Nashville: Broadman & Holman, 1994).

13. As quoted in *Great Books of the Western World*, ed. Robert Maynard Hutchins, vol. 3, "The Great Ideas: II," 915. On the idea of truth in Christian thought, see the author's *What Is Truth?*

14. C. S. Lewis, *The Great Divorce* (New York: HarperCollins, 1946), 75, emphasis original.

15. Lewis, *Mere Christianity*, 50.

Chapter 5 The Book

1. Stephen Prothero, *Religious Literacy: What Every American Needs to Know* (San Francisco: HarperSanFrancisco, 2007), Appendix.

2. This analogy has been adapted from Lee Strobel, *Inside the Mind of Unchurched Harry and Mary* (Grand Rapids: Zondervan, 1995), 115–16.

3. On this, see F. F. Bruce, *The New Testament Documents: Are They Reliable?*, 6th ed. (Grand Rapids: Eerdmans, 1984), 16–17.

4. Bruce M. Metzger, *Manuscripts of the Greek Bible* (New York: Oxford University Press, 1981), 54. Beyond these ancient Greek manuscripts, there are an additional eight thousand copies of the Latin Vulgate translation, along with other ancient manuscripts in Syriac and Coptic languages. See also Paul Barnett, *Is the New Testament Reliable?* (Downers Grove, IL: InterVarsity, 1986); Bruce, *New Testament Documents*; Josh McDowell, *Evidence That Demands a Verdict*, rev. ed. (San Bernadino, CA: Here's Life, 1979), 39–64.

5. For further study on this, see F. F. Bruce, *Second Thoughts on the Dead Sea Scrolls*, 2nd ed. (Grand Rapids: Eerdmans, 1961); Millar Burrows, *Burrows on the Dead Sea Scrolls* (Grand Rapids: Baker, 1978); Philip R. Davies, *Qumran* (Grand Rapids: Eerdmans, 1982); William S. LaSor, *The Dead Sea Scrolls and the New Testament* (Grand Rapids: Eerdmans, 1972); Charles F. Pfeiffer, *The Dead Sea Scrolls and the Bible* (Grand Rapids: Baker, 1969); Hershel Shanks, ed., *Understanding the Dead Sea Scrolls* (New York: Random House, 1992); R. de Vaux, *Archaeology and the Dead Sea Scrolls* (London: Oxford University Press, 1973); Howard F. Vos, *Archaeology in Bible Lands* (Chicago: Moody, 1977).

6. On this, see Bruce, *New Testament Documents*, 16–17.

7. As noted by D. James Kennedy, *Why I Believe* (Dallas: Word, 1980), 33. On the historical reliability of the New Testament, see C. Stephen Evans, *The Historical Christ and the Jesus of Faith: The Incarnational Narrative as History* (Oxford: Oxford University Press, 1996), as well as Craig Blomberg's contribution to William Lane Craig's *Reasonable Faith* (Wheaton: Crossway, 1994), 193–231.

8. See Joseph P. Free, rev. and exp. Howard F. Vos, *Archaeology and Bible History* (Grand Rapids: Zondervan, 1992), 75, 114, 142.

9. Free and Vos, *Archaeology and Bible History*, 16.

10. On this, see Howard F. Vos, *Archaeology in Bible Lands* (Chicago: Moody, 1977), 148. See also Free and Vos, *Archaeology and Bible History*, 57.

11. Stoyan Zaimov, "Scientists: 'Superheated Blast from the Sky' Destroyed Dead Sea Cities, Pointing to Sodom in Bible," *Christian Post*, November 25, 2018, https://www.christianpost.com/news/scientists-superheated-blast-from-the-sky -destroyed-dead-sea-cities-pointing-to-sodom-in-bible.html.

12. Free and Vos, *Archaeology and Bible History*, 108–9. For further study on the Hittites, see J. G. Macqueen, *The Hittites*, rev. ed. (London: Thames & Hudson, 1986).

13. Information gathered from an article by John Noble Wilford, "Nonbiblical Reference to King David Found," *The Charlotte Observer*, Friday, August 6, 1993, 17A. The integrity of this find was heightened by the fact that it was written by one of Israel's enemies who would have had every reason to want to ignore the reign of David.

14. James Rogers, "Rare Ancient Treasures Bearing Biblical Names Discovered in Jerusalem's City of David," Fox News, April 1, 2019, https://www.foxnews .com/science/rare-ancient-treasures-bearing-biblical-names-discovered-in-jeru salems-city-of-david.

15. Gordon Govier, "Biblical Archaeology's Top 10 Discoveries of 2018," *Christianity Today*, December 27, 2018, https://www.christianitytoday.com /news/2018/december/biblical-archaeology-top-10-discoveries-2018-israel.html.

16. James Rogers, "Major Biblical Discovery: Archaeologists May Have Found the Prophet Isaiah's 'Signature,'" Fox News, February 22, 2018, https://www.fox news.com/science/major-biblical-discovery-archaeologists-may-have-found-the -prophet-isaiahs-signature.

17. Nelson Glueck, *Rivers in the Desert: History of Negev* (Philadelphia: Jewish Publications Society of America, 1969), 31. This assertion, despite countless archaeological discoveries related to the biblical record, continues to be true to date.

18. See Josh McDowell, "Why I Believe the Scripture," *Christian Herald*, March 1982, 45.

19. For example, in Isaiah 53, it was predicted that the Messiah would be rejected, would "carry our sorrows," and pay for our sins. In verse 5 of Isaiah 53, it even says that he would be "pierced" for our transgressions, which was hundreds of years before crucifixion had been developed as a method of execution. Isaiah 53 also predicts the Messiah coming back to life after that death (v. 11). Other prophetic passages would include, but not be limited to, Psalm 22 and Micah 5:2.

20. Peter W. Stoner, *Science Speaks* (Chicago: Moody, 1969), 107–9.

21. It is my understanding that this number was first established by F. E. Hamilton, *The Basis of Christian Faith*, 3rd ed. (New York: Harper & Row, 1946), 156.

22. As calculated by Strobel, *Inside the Mind of Unchurched Harry and Mary*, 37.

23. For a good introduction to the Hebrew mindset, see Marvin R. Wilson, *Our Father Abraham* (Grand Rapids: Eerdmans, 1989).

24. On this, see Davis A. Young and Ralph F. Stearley, *The Bible, Rocks and Time: Geological Evidence for the Age of the Earth* (Downers Grove, IL: InterVarsity, 2008).

25. Ian Hutchinson, *Can a Scientist Believe in Miracles?*, quoted in Rebecca McLaughlin, "4 Reasons to Believe in the Christmas Miracle," *Christianity Today*, December 13, 2018, https://www.christianitytoday.com/women/2018/december /christmas-miracles-4-reasons-to-believe.html.

26. McLaughlin, "4 Reasons to Believe in the Christmas Miracle."

Chapter 6 The Church

1. Adapted from Jeffrey L. Coter, "Witness Upmanship," *Eternity,* March 1981, 22–23.

2. Telling the story this way, in terms of the new community, was first suggested to my thinking by the French-born professor Gilbert Bilezikian.

3. D. O. Moberg, "Denominationalism," in Daniel G. Reid, Robert D. Linder, Bruce L. Shelley, and Harry S. Stout, eds., *Dictionary of Christianity in America* (Downers Grove, IL: InterVarsity, 1990), 350.

4. Emo Philips, "The Best God Joke Ever—and It's Mine!," *The Guardian,* September 29, 2005, https://www.theguardian.com/stage/2005/sep/29/comedy.religion; for fun, watch the video on Emo's website: http://www.emophilips.com/video/video/244.

5. For more, see David Yount, *Growing in Faith: A Guide for the Reluctant Christian,* 2nd ed. (New York: Seabury Books, 2008), 302.

6. Jacobs, *Narnian,* 213–14.

Chapter 7 UnChristians

1. Snopes isn't certain this came from Gandhi (http://message.snopes.com/showthread.php?t=61900), though it acknowledges it is widely attributed to him and has been in circulation since at least the 1920s. A reference to it is made by E. Stanley Jones, *The Christ of the Indian Road* (1925).

2. Adapted from Robert Frank, "As UPS Tries to Deliver More to Its Customers, Labor Problems Grow," *Wall Street Journal,* May 23, 1994, A1.

3. Yancey, *Jesus I Never Knew,* 132.

4. Yancey, *What's So Amazing About Grace?,* 198.

5. *Mekilta de Rabbi Ishmael,* tractate *Amalek* 3.55–57 on Exod. 18:1, as cited by Darrell L. Bock, *Luke,* BECNT (Grand Rapids: Baker Academic, 1996), 343.

6. Stephanie Zacharek, Eliana Dockterman, and Haley Sweetland Edwards, "2017 Person of the Year: The Silence Breakers," *Time Magazine,* December 18, 2017.

Chapter 8 Next Steps

1. C. S. Lewis, *Weight of Glory and Other Addresses* (New York: HarperOne, 1980), 26.

2. This illustration has been adapted from *The Bridge* (Colorado Springs: NavPress, 1981) by the Navigators, as well as Bill Hybels and Mark Mittelberg, *Becoming a Contagious Christian* (Grand Rapids: Zondervan/Willow Creek Resources, 1994), 156–59.

James Emery White (PhD) is the founding and senior pastor of Mecklenburg Community Church, a suburban megachurch in Charlotte, North Carolina, often cited as one of the fastest-growing church starts in the United States. He is the president of Serious Times, Inc., a ministry that explores the intersection of faith and culture, and hosts his website, ChurchAndCulture.org, featuring his messages and blogs. He has completed advanced university study in American religious history at Vanderbilt University and continuing education at Oxford University in England, including participation in Oxford's Summer Programme in Theology. Former president of Gordon-Conwell Theological Seminary, White is the author of several books, including *The Rise of the Nones*, *Meet Generation Z*, *Rethinking the Church*, *What They Didn't Teach You in Seminary*, and *The Church in an Age of Crisis*. He lives in North Carolina.

Welcome to the first truly
POST-CHRISTIAN GENERATION

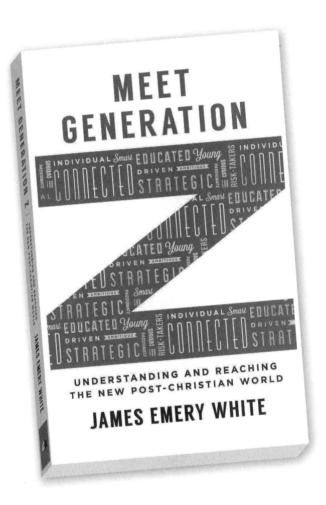

ALSO BY
JAMES EMERY WHITE

Explore
ChurchandCulture.org
BLOG | HEADLINE NEWS | RESOURCES

CHURCH&CULTURE   about   blog   **resources**   speaking engagements   contact   search

Messages by James Emery White

These are the sermon series delivered by James Emery White at Mecklenburg Community Church. For your convenience, you'll find them organized by category. Messages are available in .mp3 or .pdf formats; in the latter format you'll find the entire written manuscript including programming notes should you wish to develop a similar set of sermons.

Current Series:

CHURCH&CULTURE   about   blog   **resources**   speaking engagements   contact   search

Here's what's happening on the church and culture front today...

Amazon's Alexa could soon have opinions and make decisions for you

At Amazon's re:MARS conference in Las Vegas last week, Jeff Bezos unveiled a flurry of startling new technologies which offered a glimpse into the future the Seattle-based company is dreaming up for consumers. (Boland, *The Telegraph*)

Read more>>

Jun 13, 2019

Sex-abuse allegations grow against Catholic clergy in Poland

The Catholic Church in Poland has seen an uptick in accusations from people claiming to have been sexually abused by clergy as children, after a YouTube video sparked public anger at an institution that is at the political and social heart of this culturally conservative country. (Hinshaw, *The Wall Street Journal*)

Read more>>

Jun 13, 2019

CHURCH&CULTURE   about   **blog**   resources   speaking engagements   contact   search

The Real Challenge of Millennial Giving

June 13, 2019

"Millennials want to give to a cause."

Heard that one? Of course you have. And it's true. Just not the whole truth.

Here's all of it:

EVERYBODY wants to give to a cause.

It's just Millennials who are holding the church accountable to having one (which, I might add, is a good thing). So how have many responded in a knee-jerk fashion? By creating "boutique" giving options that offer channeled, specific giving to direct "causes" that bypass the general operating budget of a church or nonprofit.

So instead of giving to a general operating budget that might result in, say, a desk or a laptop or a 401K for field workers (no "cause" there, right? Just that damnable, wicked, evil "overhead."), you can give to drilling a specific water well outside of Lusaka, Zambia that will serve 112 AIDS orphans.

Pure, unadulterated "cause" giving.

So quick, which one do you want to give to—the "overhead" desk or the water well?

And all God's people said, "Water well."

Here's the problem. That water well won't be dug without a desk. Meaning a person on the field, in that area, serving as a liaison between your money and the actual completion of digging that well. Not to mention identifying the AIDS orphans who will be served.

The desk IS the water well.

How do I know?

To carry our example out, I personally traveled to Lusaka, Zambia. Our church had just sponsored

Search Posts

🔍 Search

Post Archive ⌄

Subscribe

Sign up to receive the twice-weekly Church & Culture blog delivered straight to your email account.

Email Address

SIGN UP

We respect your privacy. Please refer to our Privacy Policy for more information.

Featured Posts

LIKE THIS
BOOK?

Consider sharing
it with others!

- Share or mention the book on your social media platforms.
  Use the hashtag **#ChristianityforPeopleWhoArentChristians.**

- Write a book review on your blog or on a retailer site.

- Pick up a copy for friends, family, or anyone who you think
  would enjoy and be challenged by its message!

- Share this message on Twitter, Facebook, or Instagram:
  I loved **#ChristianityforPeopleWhoArentChristians by**
  @JamesEmeryWhite // @ReadBakerBooks

- Recommend this book for your church, workplace,
  book club, or class.

- Follow Baker Books on social media and tell us what you like.

 ReadBakerBooks

 ReadBakerBooks

 ReadBakerBooks